The
Table Saw
Book

The
Table Saw
Book

KELLY MEHLER

The Taunton Press

for fellow enthusiasts

© 1993 by The Taunton Press, Inc.

First printing: September 1993
Printed in the United States of America

A FINE WOODWORKING Book

FINE WOODWORKING® is a trademark of The Taunton Press, Inc.,
registered in the U.S. Patent and Trademark Office.

The Taunton Press, 63 South Main Street, Box 5506, Newtown, CT
06470-5506

Library of Congress Cataloging-in-Publication Data

Mehler, Kelly.
    The table saw book / Kelly Mehler.
       p. cm.
    "A Fine Woodworking book"—T.p. verso.
    Includes index.
    ISBN 1-56158-011-2
    1. Circular saws. 2. Woodwork. I. Title.
TT186.M45   1993   93-22422
684'.083—dc20   CIP

This book is dedicated to my entire family but especially to my wife, Teri, and our two children, Jason and Lisarose, for their love, support and encouragement throughout my woodworking career.

ACKNOWLEDGMENTS

More than a few people at The Taunton Press, both past and present,
have had a hand in this book, directly and indirectly. They have all been
amazingly supportive, and nicer people would be hard to find. Rick
Mastelli, Tom Menard, Craig Umanoff, Sandor Nagyszalanczy, Charley
Robinson, Jim Cummins and Dick Burrows have all guided me toward
this publication. Andy Schultz has been my editing mentor and my main
collaborator on this project. The excellent photography is from the
camera of Dick Burrows, a friend, author and fellow woodworker.
A special thanks to Mark Duginske for his friendly advice.

A number of representatives from various companies have helped me
with technical as well as general table-saw information, including Roger
Thompson (Biesemeyer Mfg. Corp.), Larry Olson, Mark Schiefer and
Matt Ross (Delta), Phil Humfrey (Excalibur), Roy Baker (Powermatic),
Kurt Wilke (Wilke Machinery), Tony LaClair (General), Gary Chinn
(INCA-Garrett Wade), Brad Witt (Woodhaven), Tim Hewitt (HTC) and
all the folks at Vega.

And finally to the patrons of my woodworking business, a special thanks
for their patience and insightful understanding during the painfully slow
process of writing this book.

CONTENTS

Introduction   **1**

CHAPTER 1
Table Saws   **2**

Types of saws   **2**

The parts of the table saw   **6**

Standard safety equipment   **13**

Which saw should you buy?   **14**

CHAPTER 2
Sawblades   **18**

Types of blades   **18**

The parts of the sawblade   **21**

Specialty blades   **26**

Flanged collars   **29**

Blade maintenance   **30**

CHAPTER 3
Setting Up a Space   **32**

Saw setup and placement   **32**

Workflow   **34**

Lighting   **34**

Wiring   **34**

Dust collection   **37**

Shop accessories   **41**

Shop tools   **45**

CHAPTER 4

Adjustment and Maintenance 48

Base 50

Table surfaces 50

Sawblade 51

Rip fence 56

Splitter 58

Miter gauge 59

Throat plate 60

Internals 62

Cleaning and lubrication 66

CHAPTER 5

Safety 68

Kickback 70

Safety accessories 74

Ear protection 83

Dust protection 85

Eye safety 88

First-aid procedures 90

CHAPTER 6

Ripping   92

The rip fence   92

Standard ripping   100

Ripping long stock   104

Ripping sheet stock   107

Ripping narrow stock   109

Ripping short pieces   111

Ripping thin stock   112

Ripping thick stock   112

Resawing   114

Ripping irregular stock   114

Ripping at an angle   115

Ripping an unsurfaced board   116

Ripping bevels   116

Cutting coves   117

CHAPTER 7

Crosscutting   120

Miter gauge   120

Sliding crosscut box   124

Standard crosscutting   127

Repetitive crosscutting   129

Crosscutting wide panels   133

Crosscutting short pieces   134

Crosscutting bevels   135

Crosscutting miters   136

CHAPTER 8
Table-Saw Joinery

Table-Saw Joinery 140

Edge joints 142

Rabbets, dadoes and grooves 148

Lap joints 159

Mortise and tenon 163

Finger joints 167

Miter joints 171

Sources of Supply 174

Index 177

INTRODUCTION

The table saw is the most important power tool in my workshop, yet it is a machine that is easy to take for granted since its mechanical operation seems so simple. It has taken me quite a few years to figure out how to get the most out of this versatile tool, and this book is my attempt to pass on some of the knowledge I have acquired along the way.

The book covers all the basic areas of table-saw use, with extensive discussion of ripping, crosscutting and maintenance. I've also included chapters on sawblades and setting up a work area for your table saw. Although table saws come in many makes, models and sizes, I have tried throughout to show procedures and techniques that are general enough to work on any saw.

What you won't find here is discussion of such operations as gouging out bowls, cutting circles, resawing wide stock and shaping on the table saw. These operations, which are often recommended in old woodworking books, are inefficient at best and plain dangerous at worst. There are usually better ways to do the same operations without taking unnecessary risks.

Safety is a very important issue in my shop, and I have devoted a substantial amount of space here to reinforce safety habits at the table saw. Through 20 years of experience, I have gained great respect for the table saw, not only for its creative capabilities but also for its destructive potential.

One of the things that makes my work as a custom furniture maker so enjoyable is when parts of a project fit together to make a good joint. I rely heavily on the table saw, not only to cut parts to precise width and length but also to cut the majority of my joinery. In the final chapter of this book, I present several joints that can be cut on the table saw. Along the way, I describe a number of shopmade jigs and accessories that you can incorporate into your work for safer, smoother and more efficient table-saw operation.

CHAPTER 1
Table Saws

The table saw is one of the most important and versatile power tools in the woodshop. Every piece of wood that goes into a woodworking project is cut to width and length, and the various pieces are joined to each other in different ways. The table saw is the tool that will allow you to rip, crosscut and join wood most efficiently. If you are new to the craft of woodworking, a table saw may quite likely be your first major power tool; if you are a more advanced woodworker, you may be looking to learn more about the saw or to research a particular detail. In this chapter we'll discuss various types of saws and look at the functions of standard table-saw parts, all of which will help you get a better understanding of how the saw works.

Types of saws

Table saws are marketed for various levels of use and expertise. There are saws for the home hobbyist, the carpenter or contractor, the small production shop, and large industry. But whatever the saw, the basic working principles are the same. A motor spins a circular sawblade, which protrudes through a table, and the workpiece is moved through the blade.

The Delta 10-in. contractor's saw is a popular table saw for the home shop.

Table saws can be grouped into two broad categories: motorized and motor driven. Motorized saws are saws that have the blade mounted directly onto the motor arbor. This design is not very common today, although it can still be found on some combination machines and some very small bench saws.

On motor-driven saws a motor drives the arbor by means of one or more V-belts and a pulley arrangement. Most saws today are motor driven. The most common, ranging from smallest to largest, are described below.

Bench saws

Bench saws take up little space but are still able to do much general work. Sizes for this saw run from 8 in. to 10 in. (in table saws, "size" refers to blade diameter). Because of their small table, bench saws are limited in their cutting capacity, although there are extension tables and other accessories available to increase their surface capacity. Bench saws are designed for occasional use at home and light-duty carpentry. They are portable and come without a stand.

Contractor's saws

Contractor's saws are probably the most common saws found in the home shop. They are full-sized saws with an open stand and usually a medium-weight table. Most contractor's saws are sturdy, yet they can still be moved in the shop easily. Most use standard 10-in. blades and will accept a host of accessories. Contractor's saws are adequately powered for cutting dimension lumber, but the motor often labors when cutting heavier hardwoods. The photo on p. 3 shows the Delta contractor's saw.

Bench saws are a portable, less expensive alternative to full-sized table saws. (Photo by Sandor Nagyszalanczy.)

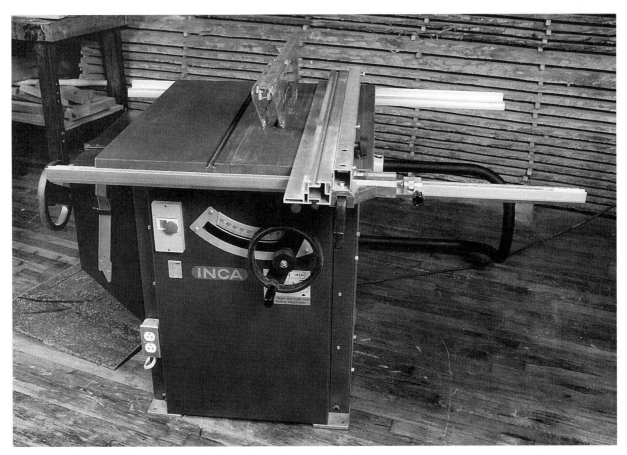

The 12-in. Inca 2100 is a professional-quality cabinet saw that is particularly well suited for furniture making.

Prices for contractor's saws range from about $400 to $800. On some of the less expensive models, accuracy is hard to achieve, because cheaper saws are made of thinner materials and are machined less precisely. Achieving accurate cuts is much less of a problem with the higher-quality (and higher-priced) saws.

Cabinet saws

Cabinet saws are rated to be professional-level machines. They are heavy, powerful and more accurate than their smaller counterparts. Not surprisingly, they also are more expensive — from about $800 to $3,000. As their name implies, cabinet saws have a fully enclosed cabinet, which the saw table is attached to. The cabinet adds heft and stability to the saw, and since it encloses the motor and internal parts it muffles some of the noise. (On contractor's saws the motor hangs off the back of the saw.) Older saws had cast-iron cabinets, but today most cabinets are of thinner stamped steel.

Industrial table saws are massive, heavy-duty machines used in intensive production work.

Industrial table saws

Industrial saws are the largest table saws available, taking from a 14-in. to an 18-in. blade. They are built for very heavy, continuous production work and commonly have a built-in sliding cast table and a cast rip fence. Some models feature hydraulic controls for fast blade-height and blade-angle adjustment.

The parts of the table saw

All table saws share standard features, although the design, materials and quality vary from model to model. These features include a base, a table, rails, a rip fence, a miter gauge, a throat plate, adjustment wheels and a power switch.

Base

The base, or body, is the part of the saw that holds up the table, either on its own (cabinet saw) or in conjunction with a stand (contractor's saw), at a comfortable working height—about 34 in. The base also holds the adjustment wheels and power switch and can enclose the sawdust-collection area (see pp. 37-39).

Parts of the Table Saw (Exterior)

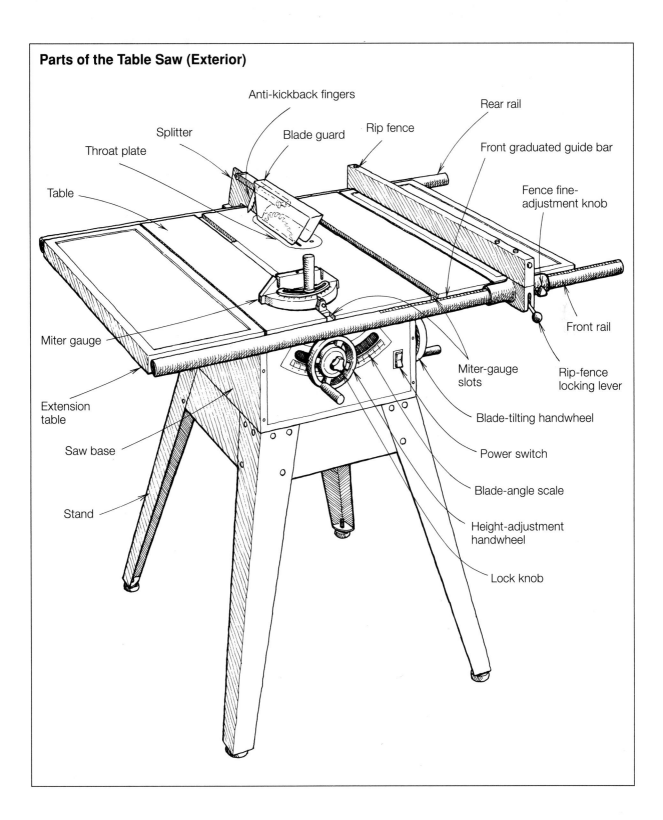

Anti-kickback fingers

Splitter

Blade guard

Rip fence

Rear rail

Front graduated guide bar

Throat plate

Fence fine-adjustment knob

Table

Miter gauge

Front rail

Extension table

Miter-gauge slots

Rip-fence locking lever

Saw base

Blade-tilting handwheel

Stand

Power switch

Blade-angle scale

Height-adjustment handwheel

Lock knob

Table

The table is the working surface that the workpiece rides on. For the saw to cut correctly, the saw table must be perfectly flat. On most machines the table top is made of cast iron, but it also can be made of stamped sheet steel or cast aluminum. Extension tables to either side can be made of the same materials. Machined into the saw table are the miter-gauge slots and the cutout for access to the blade, which is covered by the throat plate (see p. 10).

Rails

Most saws have rails attached at the front and rear of the table. The rails not only support the fence but also help support the side extension tables. On most saws the front rail has a gauge that shows the distance from the fence to the blade. Some saws have only a front rail for the fence to ride on. These saws are best suited for light-duty work, unless the fence has a very wide T-body to ride the front rail. On saws without a rear rail, the back of the fence has to be clamped in place to keep it from deflecting while making a cut.

The length of the front and back rails determines the ripping capacity of the saw. Many saws offer longer rails as add-ons; these are handy, especially for cutting sheet goods. Some table saws have sliding rails that can be adjusted to the left or the right to give maximum cutting capacity to either side of the saw.

Rip fence

The rip fence, set parallel to the blade and the proper distance from it for the width of cut desired, guides the workpiece during ripping operations. At its front, the fence has a clamp lever that locks the fence to the rails. It works by means of a cam that pushes against the front rail when the lever is depressed and at the same time pulls on a rod that tightens a J-clamp on the rear rail (if the saw has one). Some fences also have a micro-set knob at the front for finer adjustments—a handier solution than trial-and-error tapping the fence one way or the other.

You can upgrade your saw with any number of optional fence "systems" for added cutting capacity and/or improved performance (these after-market fences are discussed in detail on pp. 97-99). Replacement-fence systems generally cost a lot less if you buy them as part of a table-saw package.

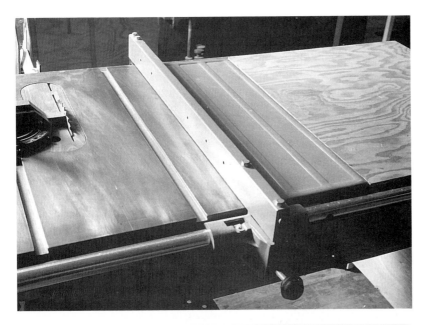

The rip fence guides the workpiece through the sawblade during ripping.

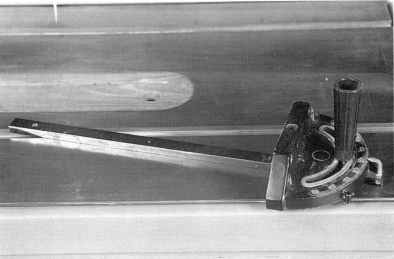

The miter gauge guides the workpiece through the sawblade during crosscutting, usually at 90° to the blade.

Miter gauge

The miter gauge is used to guide the workpiece during most crosscutting operations, usually at 90°. The miter-gauge body pivots, and most models have adjustable stops at 90° and 45° as well as a calibrated protractor scale marked on their body. A locking knob can set the protractor body at any angle between 30° and 90°. (The gauge usually can't be set at less than 30°.)

The miter gauge slides in the slots milled into the table top, to the left and right of the blade. Some miter-gauge guide bars are T-shaped in section to fit matching T-slots in the table. This configuration keeps the miter gauge from lifting out of its slot when pulled out in front of the saw.

Some European-style miter gauges come with an adjustable extruded fence facing, which provides greater support for the workpiece. These miter gauges also are usually equipped with adjustable drop stops, which ride in a T-channel in the top of the body.

Throat plate

The throat plate, or table insert, is made from soft die-cast metal that won't damage the teeth on the sawblade if they come into contact with it. The plate has an opening for the blade, which is wide enough for the blade to pass through when tilted at 45°. There is also a narrower opening at the back of the throat plate to accommodate the splitter. Generally, the throat plate has leveling screws to adjust its position relative to the table top (see pp. 60-61). It may also have a screw for securing it in the table.

Adjustment wheels

Changes in blade height and angle are accomplished by means of handwheels attached to the saw base. The *height-adjustment hand-wheel* is located under the front of the saw (see the photo on the facing page). The handwheel is used to raise and lower the blade and can be locked in place with the knob located at its hub. The Inca has a unique height gauge at the front of the saw.

The *blade-tilting handwheel* is usually located either on the right or left side of the saw base. It is used to tilt the blade for miter cuts and to set the blade at 90° to the table top for square cuts. The handwheel has a corresponding degree gauge, usually on the front of the saw base, that gives the approximate angle of cuts (a pointer moves along with the arbor). Like the height-adjustment handwheel, the blade-tilting handwheel has a locking knob at its hub.

Power switch

Accessibility is a major consideration for the placement of the on/off switch. You want to be able to turn the machine off quickly in an emergency, and to turn it on easily when handling larger work. You don't want it to be turned on accidentally. On my saw I installed a knee switch (see p. 36), which I like since it lets me turn the saw off without having to take my hands off the work. Some woodworkers like to mount the switch on a post above the saw. You should feel free to investigate any alternative switch placement that makes the saw easier for you to use.

The handwheel at the front of the saw raises and lowers the blade. The magnetic power switch (at right) is a good safety feature on larger table saws.

A magnetic switch is safer and more responsive than a toggle switch. It has two large buttons and will cut the power with a light touch. A magnetic switch will turn off when there is an electric overload or when the power is disconnected and will not come back on until the on button is pushed. Magnetic switches come standard on many large saws and are a good safety option for others.

Internals

Underneath the saw table lie the simple parts and assemblies that allow the motor to transmit power to spin the sawblade (see the drawing on p. 12). A good understanding of how these parts work together is essential for maintaining a well-tuned saw.

The *trunnions* at the front and rear of the saw support the cradle assembly and allow the blade to be tilted. On contractor's saws the trunnions are bolted to the underside of the table. On cabinet saws they are secured to the cabinet itself.

The *cradle assembly* rides in channels or ways milled into the trunnions. The cradle supports the *arbor assembly,* which consists of a metal piece with two support bearings for the arbor.

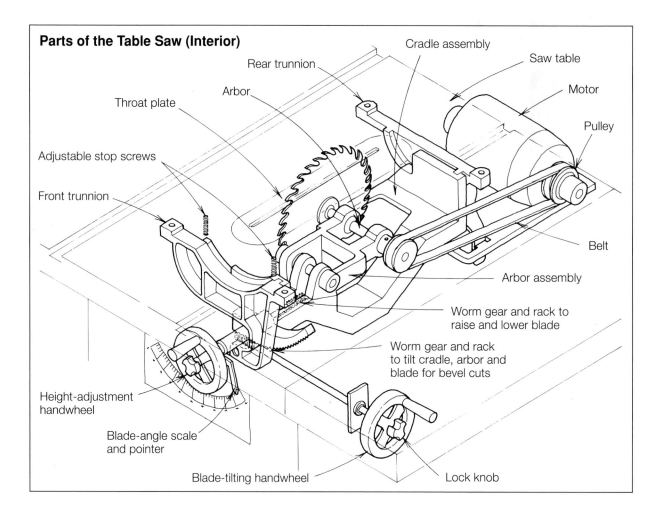

Parts of the Table Saw (Interior)

Cradle assembly

Rear trunnion

Saw table

Arbor

Motor

Throat plate

Pulley

Adjustable stop screws

Front trunnion

Belt

Arbor assembly

Worm gear and rack to raise and lower blade

Worm gear and rack to tilt cradle, arbor and blade for bevel cuts

Height-adjustment handwheel

Blade-angle scale and pointer

Blade-tilting handwheel

Lock knob

The **arbor** is a metal shaft. One end, which is threaded, holds the sawblade. The other end has a single or multiple pulley that allows the arbor to be driven by means of a motor and belt(s). Small table saws may have a ½-in. diameter arbor, but on most saws the arbor size is ⅝ in., which is sturdier and runs more smoothly. Higher-quality table saws may have larger-diameter arbors. On some oversized arbors, the end of the shaft is turned down to fit the standard sawblade arbor holes (⅝ in. or 1 in.).

Both the cradle assembly and the arbor assembly have **rack gears.** The blade-tilting handwheel and the height-adjustment handwheel turn rods with worm gears on their ends that engage the rack gears, allowing the blade to be raised, lowered and tilted. On most saws, an **adjustable stop** at either end of the rack gears allows the blade-tilting mechanism to stop at exactly 45° and 90°.

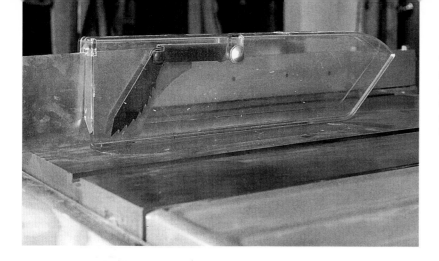

The standard splitter and guard assembly on the contractor's saw consists of a thin piece of metal directly behind the blade, and a see-through plastic hood that fits over the blade.

Standard safety equipment

The table saw is a simple machine, but the potential for accidents is great. For this reason, certain safety features are built into the saw and sold as standard equipment. These include blade guards, splitters, anti-kickback fingers and belt and pulley guards. For a more detailed discussion of safety features, see pp. 74-83.

Blade guard

The blade guard covers the sawblade and helps to prevent your hands from accidentally meeting it. It also keeps wood from dropping onto the blade while the saw is running, and deflects the chips and sawdust that are thrown from the cut toward the operator. The guard can be made from shaped clear plastic or a combination of metal and plastic, although some guards on industrial saws are made entirely of metal. A good guard covers the blade, allows undistorted visibility and usually rides on the stock. It should be wide enough to cover a tilted blade but not so wide that it will trap small cutoffs between its sides and the blade. If the guard that comes with your saw is unsatisfactory, consider purchasing an after-market guard (see pp. 77-79).

Splitter

The splitter (also called a spreader or riving knife) is a piece of metal slightly thinner than the blade. It is located directly behind and in line with the blade, and its design varies from model to model. The main function of the splitter is to keep the saw kerf in the workpiece from closing up after the cut and then grabbing the blade and throwing the workpiece back at you. The splitter also prevents the wood from coming away from the fence onto the rear of the spinning blade, where it can be picked up and thrown, or kicked back (for more on kickback, see pp. 70-74). It's not only the flying wood that can hurt you; your hand can also be pulled into the blade. The splitter is as essential a piece of safety equipment as the blade guard.

Anti-kickback fingers attached to the splitter allow the workpiece to slide forward during ripping but resist travel in the opposite direction in case of kickback.

Anti-kickback fingers

Anti-kickback fingers (or anti-kickback pawls) allow the workpiece to pass under sharp teeth while it is being pushed forward but they will dig into the wood if it starts to travel in reverse. The anti-kickback fingers are usually attached to the splitter but sometimes are part of the guard. In order for the anti-kickback fingers to do their job they must be kept sharp, yet not scratch the wood as it passes under them. Since you'll be cutting wood of different thicknesses, the fingers need to be adjustable. European safety standards don't require anti-kickback fingers, since most European saws use a different style of fence to prevent kickback (see pp. 95-97), in combination with a splitter.

Belt and pulley guard

On contractor's saws, where the motor is exposed, a belt and pulley guard keeps objects (and fingers) from getting caught up between the belt and the pulley. Sometimes the guard requires adjustment relative to the pulley placement on the motor shaft.

Which saw should you buy?

Over the years, I have owned or used many table saws. I have gone from attaching a sawblade under a piece of ¾-in. plywood to an 8-in. $49 saw, to a small 2-hp saw, and finally to my current table saw, a 10-in. 3-hp three-phase cabinet saw. I think I can honestly say that even though the quality of my work has gotten better with experience, it was not a direct result of my table saw. Tuning up your saw, buying or making a better fence and safety system and working within the saw's capabilities can give you good results. A better saw just makes it easier to get good results and is more enjoyable to work with.

Table saws are not cheap, so making a wise choice is important. First consider the type of work you want your saw to do and how often you'll be using the saw. Then weigh these considerations against the money you have to spend.

Weight

One of my earliest woodworking teachers told me that you can base the value of a woodworking machine on its weight: the heavier the tool, the better. Extra mass on old cars may be wasteful, but not on machinery. Lighter machines can vibrate more, causing parts to wear and to jiggle noisily out of alignment. A heavier machine is less prone to these problems.

This is not to say that it takes a bigger, heavier or more expensive saw to be able to do fine work. Some of today's newer saws have cast-aluminum saw tables and fences. If close tolerances are adhered to in the other mechanical systems on the saw, added mass is less imperative. I have seen some of the most beautiful and precise work come off the smallest and least expensive of tools. You can always enhance your machine to work better, and you can get to know the areas where it is deficient and work around them.

Saw size and horsepower

Most table saws for the small woodshop range from 8 in. to 12 in., with 10 in. the most common. A 10-in. saw is designed and built to handle a 10-in. blade or smaller. It takes more power as well as more bulk to handle larger blades, not only to drive them but also to cut through the thicker woods that their added diameter can handle.

Experience has taught me that a 1½-hp motor is the smallest acceptable on small saws. On saws 10 in. and up, 2 hp to 3 hp will keep the machine from being underpowered; and for a 12-in. saw, you need at least 3 hp.

A word of warning: when you are choosing a motor, beware "peak" horsepower ratings. Peak horsepower is the maximum horsepower reached with no load. "Rated" horsepower is more relevant since it is the horsepower you get with a load. An easy way to distinguish the two is to look at the amperage rating on the motor. (For further discussion of electrical requirements for your table saw, see pp. 34-36.)

Workload

Think about the kind of work you will be doing and how seriously you will be using your saw. The quality and weight of the saw, its table size and fence, and the motor's horsepower can make a big difference in how you are able to handle the work.

For example, if you'll be cutting a lot of plywood, you'll need a large table surface, a 24-in. rip capacity and a sturdy long fence, but not a lot of horsepower. If you'll be cutting 2-in. thick hardwoods, you will need at least a 1½-hp motor; 2 hp to 3 hp would be even better. If you'll be building small toys or miniatures, however, a saw over 8 in. would be overkill.

For a serious home shop doing cabinet work of any size I would recommend a 10-in. saw with a 2-hp motor. This saw can handle a wide range of work, including cutting through a green 2x4 or an 8/4 piece of hardwood with very little bogging down. For a large commercial shop, a 10-in. to 12-in. saw with a 3-hp motor will take care of just about any task you might be doing.

As a furniture maker, I am willing to pay for features that will make for accurate work. The motor needs enough horsepower (at least 3 hp) for ripping thick hardwoods. The arbor assembly must be easily adjustable and must hold its alignment to the table. The saw table and extensions must be truly flat. The rip fence must be rigid and able to be set precisely and stay in position during use; look for a dependable measurement gauge and an accurate micro-adjust. The base and top must be solidly connected. (Portability is not an issue for furniture work.) A few European machines, such as the Inca, have been built specifically for furniture work.

Cost considerations

Since table saws are used so much in the shop, it makes good sense for professional woodworkers to invest in a machine that will be a pleasure to use and give trouble-free results. Unfortunately, these days it is hard to buy a lot in the way of real quality and craftsmanship for under $1,000. You can get a decent saw for between $1,000 and $2,000, but for the better machines expect to pay at least $2,000.

Even though not everyone can have a top-of-the line table saw, you should buy the best you can afford. As with many things, the added initial cost of higher quality usually means greater savings and more pleasure down the road.

If you buy an inexpensive saw, be prepared to spend time addressing its flaws and shortcomings as soon as you unpack it. A fair amount of fine tuning may be required to make your saw perform well, and you may have to spend more time maintaining the saw than you would with a higher-quality saw (see pp. 48-67). Additional setup time may be required for each cut, and you may find that you need to make or buy accessories to make the saw perform well or perform safely. And, finally, you may have to approach a project differently because of the saw's shortcomings.

Buying a used saw

If a good new saw is beyond your budget, buying a used saw can be an attractive alternative. Buying used also enables you to get much more for your money—for example, you should be able to buy a professional-quality used saw for the price of a brand-new contractor's saw. The difficult part is finding a source for used machinery.

A good place to start looking for a used saw is in the for-sale ads in the local newspaper. You might also consider putting a want ad in the newspaper or talking to woodworkers in your local community. Auctions are another possible source, and used saws can sometimes be found at new machinery outlets that take used saws as trade-ins. Used saws from dealers are usually reconditioned and may come with a limited warranty (and a higher price).

When you examine a used table saw, there are a few critical things to consider. Always check first for worn bearings or a bent arbor shaft, which are the most likely problem areas. Try to wiggle the arbor shaft; any play in the shaft means that it will have to be repaired or replaced. Then rotate the shaft and feel for roughness or tightness in the bearings. Bearings can be found to fit nearly any saw, if you can remove them and take them to a bearing outlet. Worn bearings can also indicate a damaged arbor.

Parts for most major brands of older saws are usually readily available from the manufacturer. If the manufacturer is no longer in business, parts can be made at a machine shop, but the cost may be more than the saw is worth.

Check the flatness of the table top with a straightedge or winding sticks. Cast table tops can be reground flat for about $100 if they are not too seriously damaged. Also look out for cracks in the top or base. Poke, feel and try the rip fence and adjustment wheels. And always ask to use a saw before you consider purchasing it.

CHAPTER 2
Sawblades

Blades for the table saw come in a variety of grades and materials and a bewildering array of tooth configurations. Just as in choosing a table saw, it is important to know what features to look for. Quality in sawblades is certainly reflected in their price. Unfortunately, not even the very best sawblade can make up for the deficiencies of a cheaply made table saw. The condition of the table saw, the sawblade and the work being done need to be matched up. A table saw that is in poor condition will produce rough cuts even with a good blade, whereas a tuned table saw will help you get smoother cuts even if the blade isn't of the best quality.

Types of blades

Most manufacturers make three grades of sawblades: industrial grade, contractor grade and consumer grade.

Industrial-grade sawblades are made to close tolerances and high standards so that they can endure the fast and continuous pace of a heavy production shop. The time and labor it takes to manufacture these blades are reflected in their prices, which range from $75 to $200.

Changing a sawblade is a simple operation: with the blade wedged in position, the arbor nut can be loosened with a wrench.

Contractor-grade blades are not quite as durable as industrial-grade blades, but they are good value if you are not involved in heavy production woodworking. These blades are probably the best choice for the serious home woodworker or the small-shop professional. You can often get a good deal on contractor-grade blades from mail-order suppliers, with prices in the $40 to $75 range; some high-quality contractor-grade blades sell for $80 to $100.

Consumer-grade blades are manufactured to minimum standards, for a market that the industry thinks is interested only in buying as cheaply as possible. The blades may have pitted teeth and a rougher finish than contractor-grade blades, and they are not machined as carefully. To me consumer-grade blades are just a waste of money. They cost $40 or less, and after a couple of sharpenings they should be thrown away.

Carbide vs. steel

Nowadays almost all sawblades are either carbide tipped or all high-carbon steel blades. It was not very long ago that steel blades were the only choice for the table-saw owner. With the development of tungsten carbide, an extremely hard alloy formed by bonding tungsten, carbon and cobalt, steel blades have been almost totally replaced in the woodshop. You can still get high-quality steel blades with teeth sharper than carbide blades, but most woodworkers save these blades for very special jobs or use them just for the pleasure.

Carbide blades cost a lot more than steel blades, but the higher initial cost is more than offset by the blades' longevity, low maintenance and cutting performance. A sawblade with carbide teeth can cut smoothly up to 50 times longer between sharpenings when cutting hardwoods and up to 400 times longer when cutting man-made materials such as particleboard. So today when you are choosing a blade for your table saw it is more a matter of what to look for in a carbide blade rather than steel vs. carbide.

Set and hollow grinding

Saw teeth need to cut a kerf slightly wider than the thickness of the blade body, so that it has enough clearance to spin freely. On carbide blades the teeth are wider than the body of the blade. On steel blades this clearance is usually provided by "setting" the teeth (bending them alternately to one side or the other).

When the set wears off, the blade body will rub on the wood. You then have difficulty feeding stock into the blade. A worn blade will burn the stock and may kick the board back toward you. Before carbide, most woodworkers sharpened their own sawblades. But it takes

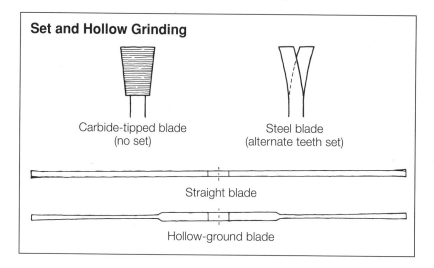

Set and Hollow Grinding

Carbide-tipped blade
(no set)

Steel blade
(alternate teeth set)

Straight blade

Hollow-ground blade

specialized equipment (diamond wheels) to sharpen carbide, so most people now send their blades to a local shop or back to the manufacturer for sharpening.

Clearance can also be achieved by hollow grinding. On a hollow-ground blade, the sides of the body are ground on a taper, leaving it thinner near the arbor hole than at the edge. A hollow-ground blade has the advantage of producing a thin kerf, which reduces waste. However, in the grinding process a support hub is left around the center of the blade, which limits the depth of cut. Blades with a hollow-ground body and a four-tooth combination tooth style (see p. 26) are known as "planer blades." These blades produce a very smooth cut and are particularly useful for cutting highly figured wood.

The parts of the sawblade

A sawblade consists of three basic elements: the body, the arbor hole and the teeth. Here are some important things to look for when you are trying to decide which blade to buy.

Blade body

The body of a sawblade is a steel plate that must be flat and stay stiff when in use. It is usually made of nickel or chrome vanadium. The steel should be ground flat. The flatter the blade, the smoother the cut and the quieter it will run. Cheap blades are merely polished or ground quickly; better blades will show fine circular grind marks from the arbor hole to the rim of the blade. Better blades also usually have slots cut in the body to allow the rim to expand without buckling as heat builds up at the cutting edge.

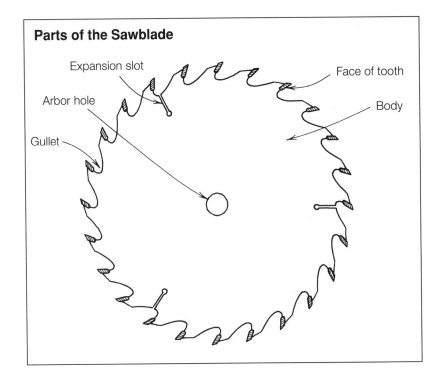

Parts of the Sawblade

Expansion slot

Arbor hole

Gullet

Face of tooth

Body

It's not easy to tell whether the blade body is flat just by looking at it. You have to try it on the saw. Blades that are not flat wobble and emit a high-pitched whine when spinning on the saw. This wobble, or deviation from the vertical, is called runout. Runout can be measured using a dial indicator and should remain under 0.005 in. If runout goes over 0.010 in. you will probably want to do something about the problem. For more on dealing with runout, see pp. 62-63.

Not all blades are made to the same thickness. "Thin-kerf blades" are smaller versions of standard blades, with thinner bodies and thinner teeth. The advantage of these blades is that they require less power to run because they remove less wood. Thin-kerf blades are well suited to bench saws and low-power contractor's saws.

Arbor hole

The arbor hole on the blade should fit as snugly as possible on the arbor, so the blade will run true. A snug fit is an indication that care was taken in the manufacture of the blade. It is easier and takes less time to make the hole oversize than to get a precise fit. If you look at the arbor hole of an inferior blade, you can see a metal lip or burr where the hole was punched. On better blades the hole is punched out undersized and then reamed to the correct fit, producing a smoother-looking hole with clean edges.

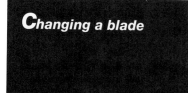

Changing a blade

Changing a blade on the table saw is a straightforward operation. First, unplug the saw. Then remove the throat plate, either by lifting it out or unscrewing the screw that holds it to the saw table. Use the wrench that comes with the saw to loosen the arbor nut. If the threads on the arbor are left-hand (as they are on most saws), the arbor nut is removed by turning it clockwise.

I wedge a piece of scrap wood under the teeth of the blade to hold the blade while I turn the nut (see the photo below). To prevent the nut from falling into the sawdust at the bottom of the saw, place your finger on the end of the arbor and unscrew the nut onto your finger.

Next remove the washer and the blade. Be sure to set the blade down on a piece of wood to prevent the teeth from chipping on the metal table. Install the new blade on the arbor, making sure that the blade's teeth face toward the front of the saw. Replace the washer and the nut. Tighten the nut lightly, again using the piece of scrap wood to hold the blade stationary. Last, replace the throat plate.

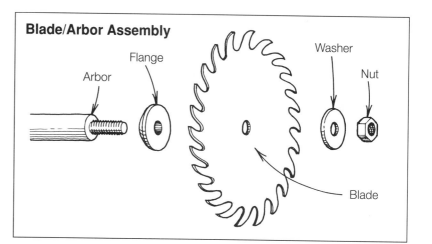

Blade/Arbor Assembly

Arbor • Flange • Washer • Nut • Blade

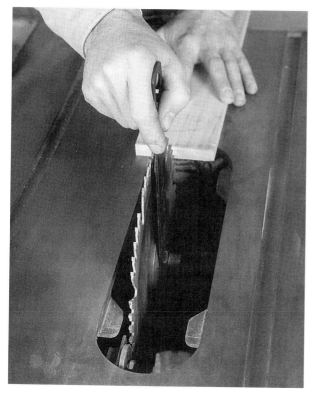

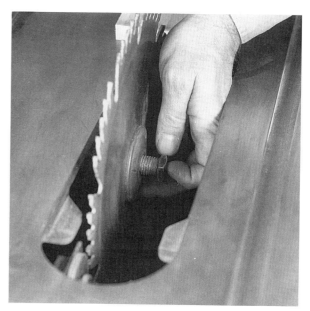

After removing the throat plate, loosen the arbor nut while wedging the blade with a piece of scrap wood (left). Screw the nut onto your middle finger to prevent it from dropping (above).

Sawblades come in various configurations for different operations. From left to right: a crosscutting blade, a blade for cutting plywood, a combination blade for crosscutting and ripping, and a ripping blade.

Teeth

Teeth are the business part of the sawblade, but more teeth does not necessarily mean better performance. Blades with more teeth get dull faster, run hotter, cut more slowly and require more feed pressure, especially when ripping. A blade with more teeth will generally produce a smoother cut, but if you edge-joint boards before gluing a glass-smooth cut isn't a necessity.

It is best to use a blade with the fewest teeth possible to get the job done. For ripping cuts (cutting with the grain of the wood), you should use a blade with from 10 to 40 teeth. Blades with more than 40 teeth are necessary only for crosscutting or cutting plywood and man-made materials, where tearout and chipping are more of a problem. Combination blades are general-purpose blades for ripping and crosscutting. Although these blades do not produce as smooth a cut as a dedicated rip or crosscut blade, the quality of cut is satisfactory and they do make frequent blade changes unnecessary.

Sawblades feature four common teeth configurations: flat-top grind, alternate-top bevel, alternate-top bevel and raker, and triple-chip grind. Each has its own particular strengths and applications.

Tooth Grinds

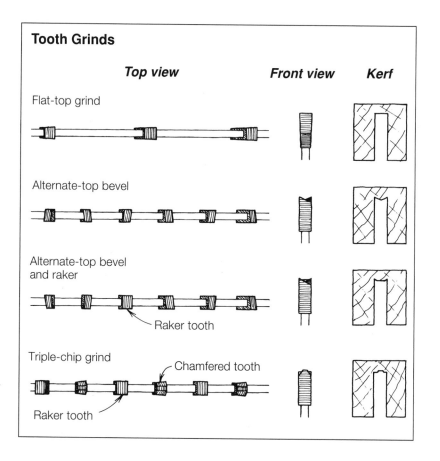

Top view   **Front view**   **Kerf**

Flat-top grind

Alternate-top bevel

Alternate-top bevel
and raker

Raker tooth

Triple-chip grind

Chamfered tooth

Raker tooth

Flat-top grind (FTG)   The flat-top grind, with teeth that have a flat face and a flat top, is the simplest tooth design. FTG teeth are primarily rip teeth and work like a chisel, cutting well with the grain but poorly across the grain. A rip blade generally has between 10 and 40 FTG teeth, with deep gullets between the teeth to eject the large chips produced. This blade takes more power to run than other types of blades, but it's the best blade to use for fast, heavy-duty ripping.

Alternate-top bevel (ATB)   The alternate-top bevel design has the tops of adjacent teeth ground at alternating angles. ATB teeth slice through the wood with a shearing action, producing a tearout-free cut across the grain. The angle of the bevel can be from 5° to 40°. The steeper the bevel, the smoother the cut but the more fragile the teeth; the shallower the bevel, the longer the teeth stay sharp. Shallow-bevel ATB blades make good general-purpose blades, working well for both crosscutting and ripping. I use a 30-tooth ATB blade for rough cutting and a high-quality 40-tooth ATB blade for cutting to final dimension.

Alternate-top bevel and raker   The alternate-top bevel and raker blade, also known as a combination blade, has groups of teeth consisting of four ATB teeth followed by one flat-top raker tooth. On a 10-in. blade there are usually 10 groups or 50 teeth. The gullets are shallow for the ATB teeth and deep for the raker teeth. This blade is probably the most commonly used general-purpose blade in the woodshop, good for both solid wood and plywood, though it is not designed for fine joinery.

Triple-chip grind   In a triple-chip grind every other tooth has its corners ground off at $45°$; the teeth in between are rakers, which can be either flat top or ATB. The chamfered tooth plows a rough center cut, which is then cleaned up by the raker. Triple-chip blades are designed for cutting man-made materials such as particleboard, plastics and aluminum, but they will do an acceptable job on solid wood as well.

Specialty blades

In addition to the standard blades described above, there are a number of specialty blades designed for specific operations. These include stacking and adjustable dado blades for cutting grooves and molding cutters for shaping the edges of boards into decorative profiles.

Dado blades

A dado is a wide groove cut across the grain in a board. To cut dadoes or other grooves at the table saw a dado head is used. Dado heads have either one or a number of blades that can be adjusted to cut a groove in a single pass. There are stacking and adjustable dado blades in either high-carbon steel or carbide tipped. Since grooving doesn't usually require very deep cutting, a 6-in. to 8-in. diameter dado set is sufficient.

The standard stacking dado head contains two types of cutting blades: outside cutters and inside chippers. The $\frac{1}{8}$-in. wide outside cutters are designed to make a smooth cut with a minimal amount of tearout. They look like a standard combination blade and have anywhere from 18 to 100 teeth. The inside chippers remove the material between the outside cutters. They have two teeth or, more rarely, four. Common sizes for chippers are $\frac{1}{16}$ in., $\frac{1}{8}$ in. and $\frac{1}{4}$ in.

By mounting chippers inside cutters in various combinations, it is possible to cut grooves from $\frac{1}{4}$ in. to $\frac{15}{16}$ in. wide, in $\frac{1}{16}$-in. increments. (For example, for a $\frac{7}{16}$-in. wide groove use two $\frac{1}{8}$-in. wide outside cutters and two inside chippers, one $\frac{1}{8}$ in. wide and one $\frac{1}{16}$ in. wide.) Fine adjustments to the width of grooves can be made by placing paper shims between the blades.

A dado head consists of two conventional-looking sawblades, chippers of various thicknesses, and paper shim stock to adjust the width of the dado.

The adjustable dado head wobbles back and forth as it spins; its angle on the hub determines the width of the dado.

Another type of dado cutting tool is the adjustable dado head, known familiarly as the drunken dado or wobble dado (see the photo at right). Either one blade (wobble dado) or two blades (V-dado) are mounted on an adjustable hub at an angle, and the pitch of the blades can be adjusted for different-width grooves. (This is the ultimate example of blade runout.)

A good-quality stacking dado set costs close to $200, but a V-dado or a wobble dado at $100 or less is more than adequate for the type of work I do (I use primarily hardwoods and not much plywood). I don't depend on these blades, since grooves and dadoes are usually more easily cut with a router. If I did a lot of dado work, I'd buy a carbide dado set from Forrest, which costs about $300 (see the Sources of Supply on pp. 174-176).

Dado heads are dangerous. They remove a lot of wood at one pass, which increases the risk of kickback. In addition, cutting with a dado head requires removal of the splitter and anti-kickback fingers. Always use featherboards, hold-downs, a pusher and a guard when working with a dado head.

Installing a dado head

After removing the throat plate and the old sawblade (see the sidebar on p. 23), install one outside cutter and then the inside chippers. If you are using two or more chippers, distribute them equally around the saw to prevent the dado head from running out of balance and causing excessive wear on the arbor bearings.

Align the inside chippers so that their cutting edges are in the gullets of the outside cutter. Correct alignment is important because the inside chippers are swaged (bent), making them thicker near their cutting edges. If this swaged part does not coincide with the gullet, the assembly will cut oversized dadoes. Install the second outside cutter and tighten the arbor nut.

Use of the dado head requires a special throat plate with an opening large enough to accommodate the full width of the head (you can make your own custom throat plate from wood, as explained on p. 61). Having the slot in the throat plate the same width as the dado head helps to eliminate tearout at the sides of the cut.

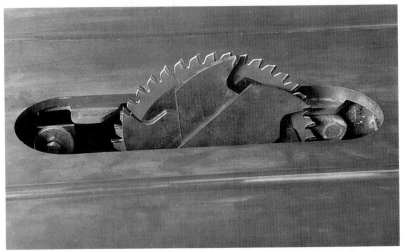

Installing a dado head is much like installing a sawblade. Put on one of the outside cutters, then the chippers and finally the other outside cutter, using shim stock as necessary between chippers. Balance the chippers so that they are equally spaced radially, with their teeth in the gullets of the outside sawblades.

Molding cutters

Molding cutters, which are used to shape stock, can be installed in a special holder (or head) that mounts on the saw arbor. Like dado heads, molding cutters are dangerous because they remove a lot of wood at one pass. In addition, the workpiece is often cut on edge, and guards have to be specially fabricated. For these reasons I advise against using molding cutters, unless you take extra safety precautions. The table saw was not designed for shaping wood — use a router or a shaper instead.

Flanged collars

True-running flanged collars, or blade stiffeners, are accessories that can enhance table-saw performance. Flanged collars installed on the arbor next to the blade give more support to the blade, which in turn reduces the vibration that can cause rough cutting and sawblade

Flanged collars add support to the sawblade, reducing the vibration that can cause rough cutting and saw fatigue. However, flanged collars also reduce the depth of cut.

fatigue. The larger the collar, the more support at the outside of the blade. Flanged collars are particularly useful for thin-kerf blades, which can flutter at the end of the cut.

Usually a single collar is installed on the outside of the blade, but you can also use two collars, one on the outside and one on the inside. When you place a stiffener between the saw's fixed collar and the blade, the blade is moved over. You may need to install a wood throat plate with a new saw slot to compensate for the thickness of the stiffener (see the sidebar on p. 61 for an explanation of how to make a wood throat plate).

Because using a flanged collar also reduces the depth of cut, it's a good idea to raise the blade with the collar until it just strikes the underside of the throat plate and note that measurement. That way you know the blade's cutting capacity. Otherwise you might forget about the collar and try to raise the blade through the throat plate while cutting a thick piece of wood. I have burned through a wood table insert (and smoked up the shop) doing just that.

Blade maintenance

A set of good sawblades can easily end up costing more than your table saw, so you'll want to take good care of them. Like other cutting tools, sawblades must be kept sharp and clean to perform at their best. Having a safe place to keep your blades with easy access to the saw is helpful. For some ideas on storing your blades, see pp. 44-45.

Keeping your sawblades sharp is the most important part of blade maintenance. Dull blades can be dangerous since they resist the work being fed into them and will degrade fast from the cycle of heat that causes gum and pitch buildup. This in turn causes more heat, and a warped blade is the usual result.

Dull blades running at high heat can also lead to cracks in the blade. A crack usually starts at the gullet and must be repaired, or the blade discarded. Blade repair is a job for the manufacturer. You might think that since carbide is so hard it would be difficult to damage, but carbide is also brittle and it doesn't take much to crack or chip it. Be careful when handling and storing carbide-tipped blades, and don't use them on any wood that may have nails in it. Inspect blades for cracks and chipped and bent teeth when you install or clean them.

Sawblades require frequent cleaning, especially when you are cutting resinous woods, such as cherry and pine. A blade gummed up with pitch on the sides of the teeth and resinous material in the gullets can reduce the blade's cutting efficiency. Either paint remover or ammonia and warm water will remove pitch and resins easily. Once cleaned, blades should be dried, then treated with a light coat of thin oil to keep them from rusting. Rust pits are as bad for the blade as pitch buildup, especially around the teeth.

CHAPTER 3
Setting Up a Space

By "setting up a space," I don't mean an entire workshop, but an ideal environment for your table saw. Some of the factors to consider are saw placement, workflow, lighting, wiring and dust collection. Once these major considerations have been dealt with, you can begin to think about shop accessories—extension tables, carts, containers for wood and scrap storage—and shop tools.

Saw setup and placement

A new table saw comes in parts, and you will first need to assemble it. Before beginning, lay out all the parts and check them against the shipping list to ensure that you got everything you paid for. Before running the saw, read the owner's manual and follow the recommendations for making all final adjustments to the saw's components. (For a detailed discussion of adjustment and maintenance, see Chapter 4.)

Place your table saw where there is adequate space around the tool, so you will be able to handle sheet goods and long boards. Ideally, you will want at least 5 ft. to the right of the blade and 4 ft. to the left, with at least 8 ft. to the front and to the rear of the blade. An area like this would give you the capacity to rip and crosscut just about any board you're likely to need for your furniture-making projects. (The usual

Set up your table saw in a well-lit, convenient location, with saw accessories close at hand and as much space around the saw as you can afford.

rule is to allow 3 ft. more in all directions than the largest piece you'll be working with.) In cramped quarters, where you can't dedicate a large space to the table saw, mobile bases can be helpful.

Ideally, it's best to locate your table saw where it can be stationary. Bolting the saw to the floor with thin rubber pads under the base helps to reduce vibration, which makes for smoother cuts. I like having my table saw face the door, so I can see visitors arrive, rather than being startled from behind while I'm concentrating on a cut.

Workflow

Consider your table saw's placement in relation to other shop tools and operations when you are setting up your shop (see the drawing on the facing page). Generally, work begins with breaking down full-sized boards into smaller pieces. Store rough lumber close to an entrance and to the milling machines that you use to work on the lumber. Work on the table saw comes after your boards are jointed and planed (see the sidebar on p. 94), so it makes sense to place your table saw near the outfeed of your thickness planer if possible.

Lighting

Lighting is a critical factor in table-saw placement. The work that you do at the table saw needs to be more precise than the work you do at the rough milling machines, cutoff saw, jointer and planer, so it makes sense to give the table saw high priority for natural light.

Overhead lighting should be placed in such a way that shadows at the saw are eliminated. You can test a proposed lighting scheme by standing a 12-in. dowel on the table-saw surface and adjusting the lighting so the dowel casts no shadow. Painting walls and ceilings white helps reflect whatever light is available. (White walls don't show up the sawdust as much as darker walls do either.)

Wiring

Once you've settled on saw size and horsepower (see p. 15), the next consideration is your wiring. Here the choice is between 110 volts (standard household wiring) and 220 volts (heavy-duty wiring), and 220 is the better choice. Your main concern should be keeping the amperage (current flow) below 14 amps. For a given horsepower rating, amperage halves as voltage doubles; for example, a tool rated at 3 hp will draw about 28 amps at 110 volts, but only 14 amps at 220 volts.

Table-Saw Placement

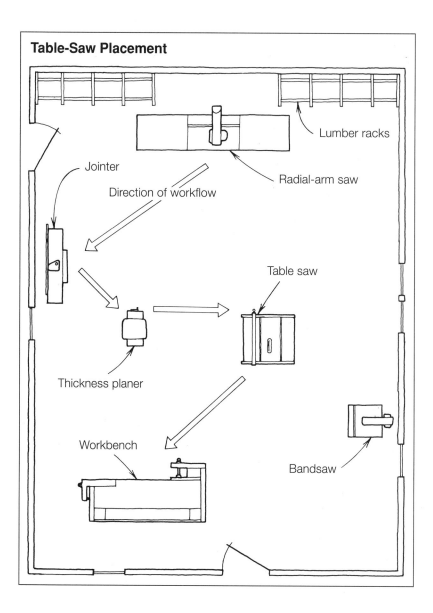

Lumber racks

Jointer

Direction of workflow

Radial-arm saw

Table saw

Thickness planer

Workbench

Bandsaw

High amperage use is hard on household current and can result in voltage drops that show up in the motor's performance. (Long extension cords cause enough resistance to produce similar results.) With 110 volts, heavier and more expensive wiring is required to the saw, and overheating and excessive wear can result. A separate 20-amp circuit for 110 volts or a 15-amp circuit for 220 is a necessity because of the high amperage use.

If you have a 220-volt outlet in your shop, most motors can easily be made to operate at either 110 or 220 voltage by changing the wire connections at the motor. Typically these connections are made at the wiring box on the motor with the nameplate and wiring instructions.

To keep from tripping over wires on the woodshop floor, it's a good idea to cover the electrical cord from the saw with a shopmade or commercial housing that has a groove in the bottom for the cord.

Knee switch

While you are dealing with electrical matters, think also about the on/off switch, and how you can improve on its design. A knee switch is a safety feature that not only makes operation of the saw more convenient but also can come in handy in problem situations. My oversized switch is a piece of wood hung from the front rail with a finger-hole cutout for access to the on switch and a block glued to the back to hit the off switch. A large off button gives a bigger target to hit when turning off your saw. I have been in a predicament where the wood I was cutting closed on the blade and I was afraid to let go of it to turn off the saw. In such situations, an off switch that can be operated by a knee or foot is a comfort. Even in ordinary use of the saw, not having to fiddle around feeling for small buttons is a great help.

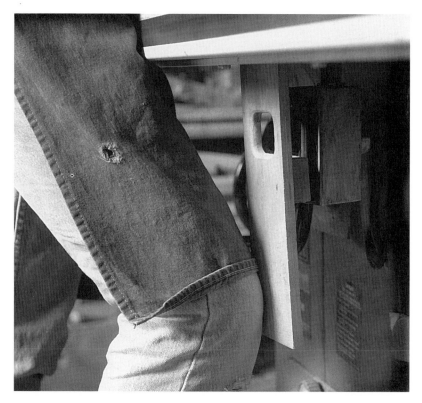

An oversized knee switch allows you to turn the saw off quickly without taking your hands off the workpiece; turning the saw on, however, requires the deliberate action of reaching through the cutout to push the button.

Dust collection

Some sort of dust collection is essential at the table saw, not only for health reasons (see pp. 85-87) but also to prevent slipping on chips and sawdust and to keep grit out of the working mechanisms of the saw. However, the table saw is a difficult machine to make dust free because it has an open structure and the blade throws dust and chips out into the air.

Most saw manufacturers have designed the possibility for a dust-collection hookup into their machines, usually in the form of open-ings or potential openings that can be adapted for fitting to a collector hose. On contractor's saws, a plate with an outlet is attached to make a floor below the table saw at the top of the stand. On cabinet models a connector, usually 4 in. in diameter, attaches over an opening either in the bottom of the cabinet or at the motor cover.

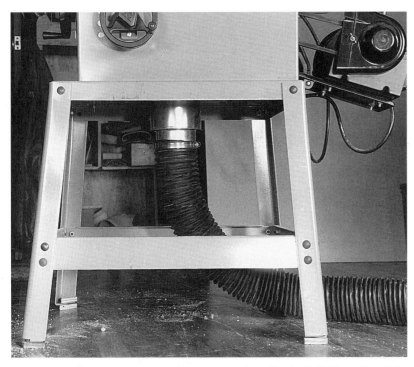

Dust collection on a contractor's saw requires the installation of a plate with an outlet at the top of the stand.

On most cabinet saws there's a hookup for a dust-collection hose at the base of the saw.

On the Inca dust-collection system, a shroud over the sawblade assembly minimizes the volume of air that needs to be removed, effectively captures most of the sawdust and keeps down interior buildup of sawdust on the parts.

On some models, such as the Inca and Powermatic's Artisan saw, the bottom of the sawblade is enclosed in order to channel the sawdust to a collector more efficiently. The Inca also incorporates an air foil that further helps channel the dust to the dust chute. With this type of system more sawdust is captured with a collector using less energy.

Sealing up the saw

On most saws, efficient dust collection depends on sealing up as much of the saw as possible. This is no small task. Ideally, you want to direct all the drawing power of the dust collector to the sawblade, where the dust is created. Begin by checking the literature that came with your table saw or request a company catalog, so that you can see what you need to do to hook up your saw to a dust collector.

On cabinet saws, you should apply silicone around the motor cover and seams. One large open area on cabinet saws is where the top attaches to the cabinet and the arbor opening. I have had good luck using duct tape around the larger openings, under the top, and around the floor on the inside of the cabinet. I slotted an inner tube and taped it to the arbor opening at the front of the saw, so very little sawdust now escapes the dust collector.

Contractor's saws are even harder to seal up. Because of their motor placement, they are left with an open back. These saws would definitely benefit from a shrouded blade, as on Powermatic's Artisan saw. Still, if you seal all other seams and openings as explained above, you will be able to collect most of the sawdust. Since most of the cutting is done with the blade at 90°, a simple removable back can help limit the spread of sawdust.

An effective way to collect dust at the sawblade is to place a hose in the saw guard and collect from above. This arrangement can be a little awkward, but it can collect a lot of the dust that is thrown from the gullets at the top of the blade. You still need to collect from below, where the majority of the sawdust goes. At least two manufacturers — Excalibur and Biesemeyer — market this type of system. The above-blade collection feature is standard on the Excalibur guard (see p. 79) and can be added to the Biesemeyer guard (see pp. 78-79) for about $70.

Choosing a dust collector

The first dust collector I considered using on my table saw was a shop vacuum. Unfortunately shop vacuums, even industrial models, cannot move enough air to be effective on any power tool in the shop. A table saw requires a minimum of about 300 cubic feet per minute (cfm) for dust collection at the point of connection. An industrial shop vacuum typically produces only about 140 cfm. A good shop vacuum produces only 100 cfm to 120 cfm and has a limited hose-diameter capacity.

For your table saw, I recommend a dust collector that is rated at 400 cfm. The smallest commercially available dust collectors have enough drawing power for the table saw, and they can do double duty as a shop vacuum.

Single-stage vs. two-stage collectors Commercially available dust collectors are either single-stage or two-stage units (see the drawing on p. 40). Single-stage systems draw sawdust directly into the blower impellers. Heavy particles drop below into a bag or other container, and fine dust is filtered up into a felt bag. Two-stage systems draw particles into a tank first, where the heavy particles are spun and drop and only the fine dust particles pass up through the impeller blades and are filtered through a dust bag.

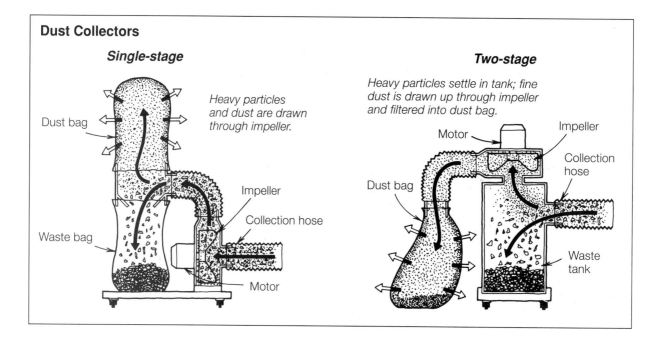

Dust Collectors

Single-stage

Dust bag

Waste bag

Heavy particles and dust are drawn through impeller.

Impeller

Collection hose

Motor

Two-stage

Heavy particles settle in tank; fine dust is drawn up through impeller and filtered into dust bag.

Motor

Impeller

Collection hose

Dust bag

Waste tank

Both types of unit have their pros and cons. Single-stage systems are generally less expensive, and since the chips and sawdust end up in an easily detachable bag they're easier to empty out. However, two-stage systems tend to last longer because there is less wear to the impeller and housing. Single-stage systems are noisier, and if metal enters the system the blades can be damaged and sparks may ignite a fire. I think two-stage systems are safer, and they're certainly easier to move around the shop than their taller single-stage counterparts.

If you are considering purchasing a dust collector, get one with fan blades made of cast aluminum, not welded sheet steel. Cast aluminum is preferred for durability and spark resistance. Also look for a collector with a quick disconnect so you can move it from machine to machine.

To set up a dust collector at the table saw, you will need a connector from your saw (usually available from the saw's manufacturer). An electric outlet connected in parallel with the table-saw motor will allow you to plug the vacuum into the motor circuit, and the dust collection will start when the table saw is turned on.

Depending on the scale of their woodshop, many woodworkers find it is usually more convenient to have a central dust-collection system hooked up to each shop machine. For information on setting up a central dust-collection system, see *Fine Woodworking* #67 (pp. 70-75) and the Delta booklet "Wood Dust Control and Collection Systems" (reprinted by Cincinnati Fan and Ventilator Co., 5345 Creek Rd., Cincinnati, Ohio 45242-3999).

Shop accessories

There are several accessories that will make your table saw easier to use. Some, such as outfeed supports, are virtually essential; others, such as carts and storage racks, are helpful. Below are some of the set-ups I've developed in my 20 or so years as a woodworker.

Outfeed supports

Outfeed supports increase the working surface of the table saw and help to keep long or wide workpieces even with the saw-table top. They are also an important safety feature (see p. 83). Outfeed supports can take many forms, ranging from a simple set of sawhorses spanned by a piece of sheet material to a plastic-laminated flat surface extending from the back and right sides of the saw. Workbenches are about the same height as the saw table, and many times I have used mine as an outfeed-support surface.

Fold-down tables and steel roller systems are available that attach to the rear of the saw and drop out of the way when not in use (see the Sources of Supply on pp. 174-176). You can also buy adjustable roller stands as separate units, but I have found these to be a liability since the rollers tend to guide the work coming off the saw away from the rip fence if they are not aligned at exactly 90° to the blade.

Commercial extension tables like these made by Biesemeyer help support the workpiece at the sides and back of the table saw.

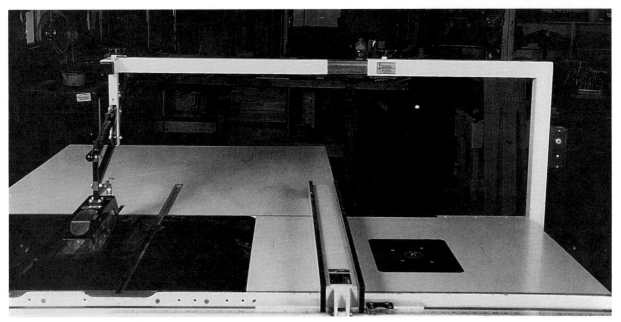

Shopmade extension tables can take many forms. Back and side extension supports cure dangerous habits like reaching across the sawblade or struggling with balancing long workpieces.

If you have the room, a larger and more permanent outfeed-support system is highly desirable. Biesemeyer offers two laminated outfeed-support systems (one professional size and one for the home shop) that are designed to attach to the back rail of its replacement rip-fence systems. The supports come with adjustable legs and are milled to match the miter-gauge slots and the standard guard assembly. Even if you don't cut a lot of sheet goods, furniture making will certainly involve handling a lot of large workpieces. I have found that the added worktop area alone has made my outfeed-support system worthwhile. I draw, assemble and test the flatness of work on my laminated top. I keep it waxed, so glue is easily removed from the surface.

If you don't want the additional expense of a commercial outfeed-support system, you can of course make your own extension tables (see the photo above). Attach a two-legged extension table to the saw table with clamps or with brackets through the guide rails. Alternatively, build a four-legged table and leave it freestanding. The outfeed support should be at the same height, or slightly below, the saw table.

Carts

Wheeled carts or tables are another helpful table-saw accessory. They can be used when moving lumber from the jointer or planer to the saw, and for holding project parts as they are being worked on and projects as they are in process.

It is quite common to be working from a stack of parts at the saw, and I find it better to work from a cart than from a pile on the saw table. (For a lot of table-saw procedures you can't have anything on the saw table anyway.) Having a place to stack parts neatly as I work on them helps me keep track of the parts more easily. A neat stack is easy to count, and missed joints are easy to see. Parts are also kept flatter when they can be stacked on a flat surface, and they are less likely to get damaged.

Wheeled carts are handy shop accessories. They can ferry lumber from the planer to the table saw, function as a portable outfeed table and even serve as a giant toolbox.

Carts are easy to come by. You can get them at furniture-factory auctions or hospital junk piles, you can recycle food carts, or you can make your own. You can even attach casters to an old table. I find it useful to have some carts that are low to the floor and some at bench height.

Racks, drums, boxes and buckets

In a well-organized workspace, frequently used table-saw tools and equipment are kept close to the saw. It's good to have a permanent spot by the saw for your push sticks, arbor wrench, miter gauge, fence, throat plates, guards, maintenance supplies and featherboards. You might also want to hang your sawblades, jigs, clipboard and patterns within easy reach of the table saw.

Some saws come equipped with braces for holding the accessories that you take on and off the most — the rip fence and miter gauge, as well as the arbor wrench. If your saw doesn't have built-in braces, they are easy enough to make in your shop (see the photo at left on the facing page).

Since a set of good sawblades can easily cost more than your table saw, it makes sense to take good care of them. I made a simple sawblade box to make better use of my wall space as well as give the blades better protection (see the photo at right on the facing page). I keep my collection of push sticks on top of this box.

Large (55-gallon) drums are handy for holding wood scraps or sawdust, and they can also be used as parts tables. I have a couple of drums that I move around the shop and even use one as a router-table base. A drum is also a handy place to set the rip fence if you have to remove it from the saw temporarily — better than the floor, where it's likely to get damaged or tripped over.

Sawdust can be swept off the table-saw surface with a bench brush, which is better than blowing with compressed air or using your hands. Sawdust, however, does not build up around the saw nearly as quickly as cutoffs. Cutoffs from the edges and ends of all your project pieces will quickly blanket the table-saw workspace. A scrap box or bucket next to the saw (not that I always hit it) helps control the mess. Pieces in the bucket go either into the 55-gallon drums and are burned in the woodstove, or they are sorted to my scrap shelves if I think they can be used later.

Arbor wrenches, miter gauges, pushers, fences and replacement throat plates can be stored on a vertical panel on the end of a side extension table.

A simple wall-hung box protects sawblades from chipping and keeps them from clanking against each other.

Shop tools

Tools needed for the table saw serve two general purposes: layout tools for measuring, marking and checking the workpiece, and tools for setting up the table-saw blade, miter gauge and rip fence for various cuts. You will be repaid many times over by investing in good tools and keeping them in good condition. Good tools enhance accuracy, and the more accurate your work at the table saw, the better your projects will turn out.

Squares and rulers are probably the tools that you'll use most at the table saw. You'll need a 6-in. try square to check fence and miter-gauge setups and the ends of your crosscuts. A machinist's combination square is handy both for checking 45° miters and as a marking gauge. A framing square is useful for checking and doing layout on larger panels and as a straightedge for confirming flatness. I carry a 2-in. engineer's square in my shop apron that is ideal for checking edges.

Check each square periodically for accuracy by placing it against the straight edge of a board and marking a line with a sharp pencil. Now flip the square on the same edge and check the blade's alignment with the mark. Any deviation from 90° will be doubled. Starrett and Bridge City Tools (see the Sources of Supply on pp. 174-176) guarantee the accuracy of their squares.

I usually carry a 6-in. metal precision ruler with metric measurements on one side and English on the other. The metric measurements come in handy for calculations because they don't involve fractions. This pocket rule will take care of much of the close work done at the saw. For longer measurements I find that both a folding rule and a tape measure have their own advantages. The tape measure hooks onto the end of a board, making it easy to get accurate measurements; a rigid folding rule is easier to handle and is better for the more exacting work of marking joinery. Because rulers often vary from each other, it's best to use only one ruler on a job. You can check your ruler for accuracy with a machinist's rule.

A pair of 4-in. sliding calipers with metric and English measurements is handy for checking thickness and sometimes narrow widths. It can be used for inside and outside measurements, and is more precise than measuring with a ruler.

I use a sliding bevel for checking and marking angles other than 90° on the workpiece, the blade and the miter gauge. I find that a gauge with the locking nut at the end of the handle is the most versatile.

Pencils are essential marking tools. I keep a #2 pencil behind my ear or in the top pocket of my apron. Heavy beginner's #308 school pencils with a lot of lead or carpenter's pencils are more appropriate for marking wood in the milling stage. I save my thin pencils for drawing on wood parts, writing and sketching.

Masking tape is indispensable in the woodshop. A few of its myriad uses include marking on the table-saw surface for rough cutoffs, leveling the throat plate, keeping small parts together, shimming jigs, fences and stops that are a smidgen out of square, and taping back chips until they can be glued back in.

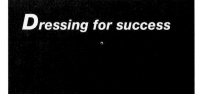
The first thing I do when I come into the shop is to put on a denim shop apron. I learned to wear a shop apron from my wife, who refuses to let me into the house when I come home with sawdust and wood chips hanging off my clothes.

Of course, a shop apron serves other purposes besides keeping most of the sawdust off my clothes and another layer away from my skin. The breast and waist pocket of the apron hold the tools that I use the most at the table saw: a pencil, a 6-in. ruler, a 2-in. engineer's square and 4-in. sliding calipers.

Shop aprons are reasonably priced at my local clothing store, and I can order a dozen aprons at a time even more cheaply. Even though I wash my aprons once in a while, eventually the glues that find their way on to them force me to throw them away.

A shop apron protects your clothes from sawdust and holds small tools as well.

CHAPTER 4

Adjustment and Maintenance

Most woodworking equipment needs periodic adjustment and maintenance, and the table saw is no exception. Regular attention to these details pays off in a saw that is dependably accurate and safe, and a pleasure to use.

The tune-up adjustments I recommend in this chapter are generally applicable to all table-saw models. However, it will be a lot easier to maintain your table saw if you keep the original instruction manual and the parts list and drawing handy. All of the parts to the tool are usually shown as they would be assembled, which can be especially helpful when doing repairs and replacing parts. If you do not have a manual and parts list, most manufacturers will send you one upon request if you give them the name, serial and model number of your saw. Manufacturers' addresses can be found in the Sources of Supply on pp. 174-176, or in the *Thomas Register* at your local library.

Many of the adjustments outlined here are periodic or one-time operations, but you should also get into the habit of checking the squareness of the blade, rip fence and miter gauge each time you go to use the saw. A single cut on a scrap piece of wood will provide a quick check for squareness.

**A table saw in prime running condition will operate smoothly and safely.
Here, the alignment of the blade to the miter-gauge slots is being checked.**

Base

A table saw needs to sit solidly on the floor, without rocking, and it should be fairly level. To adjust a saw that sits on a bolted-together stand, loosen the bolts and shift the saw in its place, with a level on the table top, until the stand makes good contact on all its supports and the top is level from left to right and front to back. Then retighten the bolts. For a saw with an enclosed base, use wedged shims strategically placed under the cabinet base.

If the base is not heavy enough the saw will need to be bolted to the floor for optimum performance, but that does of course limit your ability to move the machine. If you bolt your saw to a wood floor, check that the floor area underneath doesn't vibrate. Thin rubber pads under the saw will help reduce vibration.

Table surfaces

Before any adjustments can be made to the other parts of the saw, you need to have a flat, continuous surface to work from. The first thing to check is the flatness of the table top. You can check for twist by sighting across winding strips — two long straightedges placed on edge across the table. Minor deviations can possibly be fixed by placing shims between the top and the base. If that doesn't work, the top will have to be reground by a machine shop (at a cost of about $100). The regrinding must be light, because on some saws it can weaken the top.

Once the saw table is flat, turn your attention to the extension wings. The extension wings need to be adjusted so that they are flush where they join the main table and are also in the same plane. You can easily see if the joints are flush (see the photos on the facing page). I check and level the joint first with a short straightedge. Then I check the whole plane with a long straightedge. Place the straightedge so that it spans the table and wings completely and see where it makes contact.

If adjustment is necessary, it is best to remove the bolts that hold on the wings and clean the mating surfaces before reassembling. Tighten the bolts lightly when reassembling and maneuver each wing to make contact with the straightedge. Pressed steel wings have enough give in them to be brought back into line, and a clamp applied at the ends while tightening the bolts can help achieve a flush fit. (The clamp acts as a handle, making it easier to pull the wing surfaces into flat.) I have also encountered twist in pressed steel wings that needed further clamping where and while they were being bolted to the guide rails.

Extension wings must be level with the saw table. Check the joint first with a short straightedge (above left), and then check the whole plane with a long straightedge (above right).

Sawblade

For the table saw to work smoothly, the sawblade must be properly aligned. It must be parallel to the miter-gauge slots and perpendicular to the saw table, and it must tilt reliably to 45°.

Aligning blade to miter-gauge slots

Ideally, the sawblade should be perfectly parallel to the miter-gauge slots when the machine comes from the factory, but this is seldom the case. Many woodworkers will compensate for misalignment by adjusting the rip fence parallel to the sawblade. That solution is fine for ripping, but not for crosscutting. Even though the miter-gauge body can be angled, it still has to travel in the milled slot and therefore will never cut correctly if the blade is not aligned with it. The blade will be contacting the work at an angle and crosscutting with only the front or back of the blade. Both situations will cause binding and a rough cut, with the latter (the back of the blade cutting the work from the table up) the more dangerous. Nor will any jigs that use the slots work accurately if the blade is not parallel to the slots. Because all other adjustments use this alignment as a reference, you need to start here with the tune-up.

First, make sure that the miter bar has no side play as it slides in the miter slot (an unusual occurrence in stock gauges). The quickest and easiest way to eliminate any play in the slot is by dimpling the edges of the miter bar with a metal punch, as shown in the photo at left. This makes for a tighter fit. If the miter gauge fits too tightly, file lightly along the sides of the bar with a fine-cut file until it slides smoothly. Any burrs should also be filed lightly to avoid excessive wear in the miter slots.

A longer bar on the miter gauge will help to spread any deviation over a greater distance, making for a better fit. Some saws, like the Inca, come standard with a 30-in. bar instead of the more common 18-in. bar. You may have to stand back to insert the gauge in the slot, but you will appreciate the lack of side play in its use.

Once the miter gauge is snug, check the alignment of the sawblade and miter slot by elevating the blade to its maximum height. Clamp a ¾-in. to 1-in. square piece of hardwood to the miter gauge (it doesn't matter if the miter gauge is not at a perfect 90° angle), so that it extends about 1 in. past the sawblade. Cut the stock, turn off the power and unplug the machine.

With the end of the workpiece at either the front or back of the blade, rotate the blade (backwards so as not to remove any wood) until you find the tooth that hits the wood the hardest. Mark that tooth with a piece of chalk, as shown in the photos on the facing page, and move the stock to the other end of the blade. As you rotate the blade again,

If your miter gauge is loose in the slot, dimpling the edges of the miter bar with a punch will make it fit more snugly.

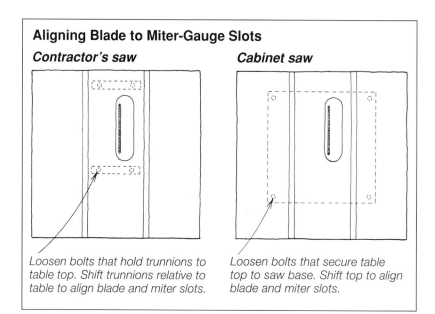

Aligning Blade to Miter-Gauge Slots

Contractor's saw

Cabinet saw

Loosen bolts that hold trunnions to table top. Shift trunnions relative to table to align blade and miter slots.

Loosen bolts that secure table top to saw base. Shift top to align blade and miter slots.

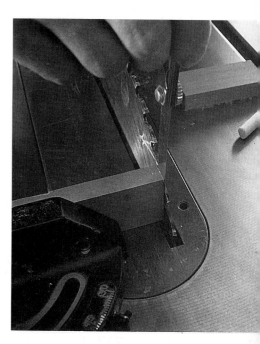

To test the alignment of the sawblade to the miter-gauge slot, rotate the blade against a test piece clamped to the miter gauge. If the blade is parallel to the slot, the same tooth should rub against the test piece at the back of the blade (above left) as at the front (above right). If the blade and slot are not parallel, use a feeler gauge to find the amount of misalignment.

the marked tooth should hit the wood and make a similar sound if the blade is parallel to the miter slot. If the tooth does not hit the stock (it probably won't), the blade and miter slot are not parallel.

To adjust the blade orientation, slightly loosen the bolts that hold the trunnions to the top or the top to the saw base, as shown in the drawing on the facing page. Now tap or shift the assembly or the table top in the desired direction (see the photo at right), then rotate the arbor and listen to the sounds the sawblade makes against the test piece. When the sounds match at the front and back of the blade, tighten the bolts and recheck. Unless the table saw is dropped, this adjustment should be a one-time procedure.

Setting blade at 90°

A sawblade in normal cutting position should be at 90° to the table. To check the 90° setting, raise the blade to its full height and place a large square on the table and against the body of the blade (between the

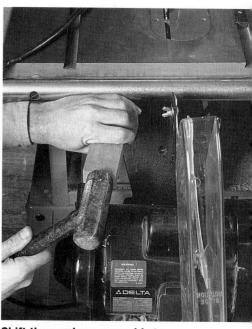

Shift the carriage assembly to realign the blade and the miter slots. Sometimes the carriage requires a little persuasion.

Use a square to see if the sawblade is perpendicular to the table.

teeth), as shown in the photo above. A more practical check, which will make up for any inaccuracies in your square or blade runout (see pp. 62-63), is with a 2-in. wide scrap of wood 18 in. to 24 in. long. Thickness is not so important, but the piece must be planed flat and square, with all opposite sides parallel to each other.

Mark a large X on the face of the board, as shown in the top drawing on the facing page. Set the miter gauge at 90°, stand the board on edge and crosscut through the center of the X with the blade at its maximum height. (First make sure that the locking knobs on the height and angle wheels are locked.) Turn off the saw. Flip one of the sawn pieces over and place the cut edges against each other. Any deviation from square will be doubled, and easy to see.

If the blade is out of square, first check the tilt mechanism. Perhaps the arbor wasn't cranked all the way to 90°, or maybe sawdust was keeping the rack from traveling all the way up to the 90° stop. If neither is the problem, turn your attention to the adjustable machine bolt that acts as the 90° stop.

Tilt the blade assembly off the stop, and loosen the lock nut on the stop bolt. Now turn the stop bolt a turn or two in the desired direction. Tilt the blade back to the stop, and repeat the cut described above until the pieces of wood match for square. When you have a good 90° position, tighten the lock nut with an open-end wrench while maintaining the stop bolt's position with a box wrench. Check the angle again, then set the blade-tilt gauge pointer at the 90° mark. The pointer is usually adjusted by loosening the screw at the front of the saw that attaches it to the arbor.

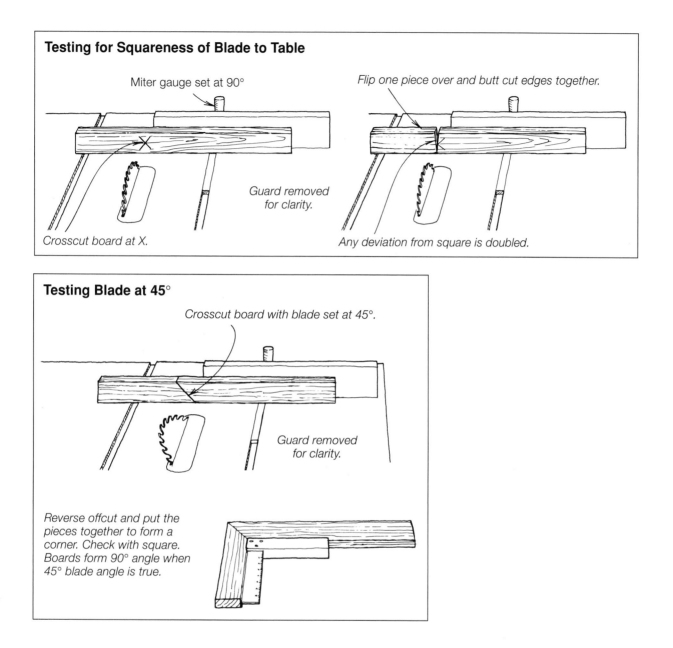

Testing for Squareness of Blade to Table

Miter gauge set at 90°

Flip one piece over and butt cut edges together.

Guard removed for clarity.

Crosscut board at X.

Any deviation from square is doubled.

Testing Blade at 45°

Crosscut board with blade set at 45°.

Guard removed for clarity.

Reverse offcut and put the pieces together to form a corner. Check with square. Boards form 90° angle when 45° blade angle is true.

Setting blade at 45°

Next, check the 45° setting on the blade-tilt mechanism, if your saw has one. Tilt the arbor to the 45° stop and cut another scrap piece on edge. Put the two pieces together as shown in the bottom drawing above; if the 45° cut was accurate, the pieces should form a 90° angle. Check by placing an accurate square on the inside of the right angle. Adjust the machine bolt that acts as the 45° stop until the two edges meet, with no gap between them.

Rip fence

A rip fence that is out of parallel with the blade will result in one of two problems. If the fence angles away from the back of the blade, it will cause the workpiece to skew away from the fence and burn the waste side of the cut. The more dangerous situation is when the fence angles toward the back of the blade. In this situation the workpiece will bind between the fence and the back of the blade, causing burning on the workpiece and potential kickback. (For more on rip-fence angle and safety, see pp. 92-94.)

The rip fence is adjusted once the blade is parallel to the miter-gauge slots. First, lock the fence in position and measure from it to the front and back of the miter-gauge slots. Alternatively, you can place one piece of $\frac{3}{4}$-in. stock at the front and another piece at the rear of the miter-gauge slot and then slide the rip fence against these to determine alignment (as shown in the photos on the facing page).

On most saws, the rip fence is adjusted by loosening the two bolts on the top of the fence and moving the fence body until it is parallel to the miter-gauge slot. An adjustment screw at the front of the fence regulates the holding power of the fence on the back rail. You may need to tighten it so that the rip fence is held snugly at the rear of your saw. Don't overtighten the screw or it will be difficult to lock the fence with the fence lock lever.

I like to set my rip fence so that it is slightly farther (about $\frac{1}{64}$ in.) from the back of the blade than from the front, so the rear teeth just miss the stock being cut. This setting gives a smoother cut and reduces the potential for kickback. Use a feeler gauge between the rip fence and a piece of stock in the miter slot at the back of the saw to measure the amount of clearance.

Cheaper rip fences of stamped steel may not be perfectly straight. If your saw has a stamped-steel rip fence, you can add an auxiliary wood fence and shim it to even out any imperfections (see pp. 94-95).

To set the rip fence, fit a couple of blocks of wood into the miter slot and slide the rip fence up against them. The fence should either touch both blocks or be ¹⁄₆₄ in. away from the block at the back of the table saw. Measure this gap with a feeler gauge (below left). Adjust the fence by loosening the two bolts on the top edge (left). Tightening the screw on the front of the fence increases the tension of the clamp on the back rail (below right).

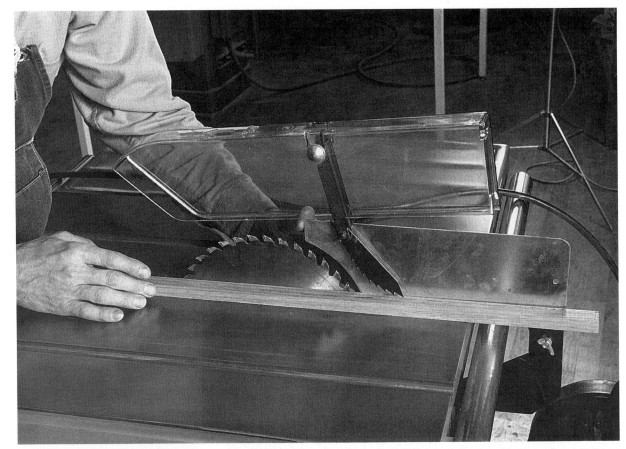

The splitter should be in a direct line with the sawblade and at 90° to the saw table.

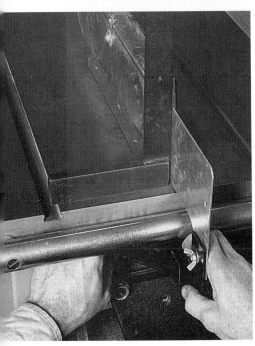

Splitter

For optimum performance and safety, the splitter must be aligned with the sawblade and at 90° to the table. A misaligned splitter may direct the workpiece either into or away from the rip fence, making it difficult to feed correctly.

It is easy enough to adjust the splitter. Loosen the bolts that attach it to the carriage assembly at the rear of the saw, and use a square for the vertical adjustment and a straightedge to line it up with the right side of the blade. Since most splitters are thin steel, if they get bent they can be twisted back into shape.

Miter gauge

An accurate miter gauge is essential for making square crosscuts and miter cuts. There are a number of ways to set the gauge to 90°. One method is to use a large square placed against the gauge and the blade body. My preferred method, however, is to crosscut a 3-in. piece off a ¾-in. by 1½-in. by 18-in. board, then turn over one of the cut pieces and put the sawn edges together against a flat surface. As when you adjusted the blade perpendicular to the table, any deviation from 90° will be doubled when you put the sawn edges together (see the top drawing on p. 55). Continue to make adjustments and cuts until the two pieces match exactly. Then set the index stop and indicator so that you'll be able to find 90° repeatedly.

To set the miter-gauge stop at 45°, adjust the gauge to approximately 45° with a protractor, a drafting triangle or a sliding bevel gauge. Then crosscut a piece of scrap wood as explained in the previous paragraph. Flip the piece, then put the pieces together to form a corner. Check this corner with a square and, once more, any deviation from 90° will be doubled. Readjust the miter gauge until an exact 45° is achieved, then set the 45° miter-gauge stop.

After squaring the miter head, use an Allen wrench to set the 90° stop.

If the 45° stop on the miter gauge is properly calibrated, you'll be able to cut a board using the 45° setting and flip one of the cutoffs to form a perfect 90° angle.

Throat plate

Most throat plates, or table inserts, have four or more adjusting screws to help level the plate with the saw table. If the plate is above the table in the front, it will prevent the work from reaching the blade; if it is below in the back, the work may catch on the rim of the opening in the table. Some woodworkers like to compensate for this situation by lowering the front and raising the back a hair. This is a good, safe practice, but I prefer to keep the plate as level as possible since some joinery operations depend on a perfectly level surface.

To level the throat plate, simply place a straightedge over the plate and adjust the individual screws until the plate is level with the table top. (Some screws adjust from the underside of the saw, some from the top.) If the throat plate does not have adjusting screws, shim it with pieces of masking tape to raise it level with the table. If the throat plate sits above the table, you may need to remove material from underneath. Better yet, replace it with a shopmade throat plate (see the sidebar on the facing page).

Once the throat plate is leveled with the table top, be sure that it does not rock. It is possible to get it level and still have an adjustment screw not touching its pad.

Turn the adjustment screws to level the throat plate.

Making a wooden throat plate

The stock throat plates that come with the table saw are not always suitable for job-specific cuts, so I prefer to make my own wooden replacement inserts. As well as ensuring a snugger fit in the table top, a custom wooden throat plate allows you to reduce the opening between the blade and the plate, which is an important safety consideration when ripping very narrow stock. A narrower opening in the throat plate also minimizes tearout at the sides of the cut.

I make my throat plates out of just about any hardwood that's available in the shop, but avoid stock with figure or defects to ensure stability. The first step is to plane the stock to exactly the right thickness so that it will be level with the table top. It's handy to have a number of throat plates with different-sized openings for different blades, so once you have the correct thickness set at the planer run extra stock for additional throat-plate blanks.

Measure the throat-plate opening in the table top and rip the stock to width. I don't use the throat plate that comes with the saw for an accurate width measurement because stock plates tend to be undersized. I do use it, however, to draw the profile for the rounded ends. Bandsaw close to the layout line,

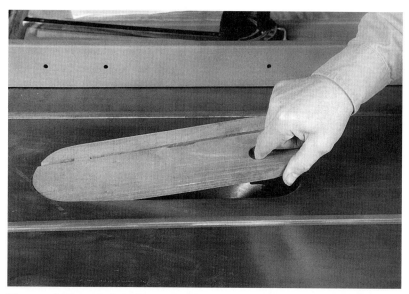

Shopmade throat-plate inserts with slots the exact size of the saw kerf make dadoing and miter cuts safer. A 1-in. finger hole is handy for removing the throat plate from the opening in the saw table.

then use a belt sander on edge for final fitting. A trial fit will leave marks on the insert where additional sanding is necessary. Go slowly until the fit is snug. You may also need to relieve the bottom edge of the throat plate to get it to seat properly in the table opening.

I like to drill a 1-in. finger hole in the front of the throat plate so the plate is easy to remove from the table. Ease the edges around the hole for smoother handling.

To make the saw kerf in the throat plate, hold down the blank with a narrow board clamped across its top and clear of the blade. Turn on the saw and raise the blade slowly. On some saws the standard blade does not go down far enough into the table to

allow you to insert the throat-plate blank. In this case, use a smaller-diameter blade to start the kerf and then switch to the desired blade and finish raising the blade through the plate. Finally, mark the splitter slot in line with the saw kerf and cut with a bandsaw or coping saw. Apply finish or wax to the throat plate to minimize wood movement.

To prevent the plate from lifting out of the table opening, you can drill and tap for screws in the platform tabs that hold the plate. I have also found that a small wood catch screwed under the back of the throat plate will keep it from lifting up at the back.

Internals

As with any other machine, the working parts of the saw—the arbor, bearings, V-belts and pulleys—need periodic inspection, cleaning, adjustments and replacement.

Arbor and bearings

The table-saw arbor needs very little maintenance, but it should be checked for wear, burrs and any play in the bearings that the arbor rides in.

With the saw unplugged and the blade removed, first check the interior flange and the arbor threads for dirt, burrs or raised nicks. Imperfections can be removed carefully with a fine-cut file. To check the bearings, turn the arbor by hand while feeling for any roughness. Grasp the arbor and gently pull up and down to check for any slack in the bearings. Roughness or slack in the bearings means they need to be replaced.

Any wear or looseness in the arbor or bearings will inevitably result in runout, which causes the sawblade to wobble and cut a wider kerf than the width of the blade. Runout can also occur when the arbor flange is not at exactly 90° to the arbor. To measure runout in the flange, hold a dial indicator against the flange and rotate the arbor. Runout should be less than 0.010 in. More than 0.010 in. will cause enough vibration at the edge of the sawblade to cause rough cutting as well as splintering (especially with sheet stock), even with the best of

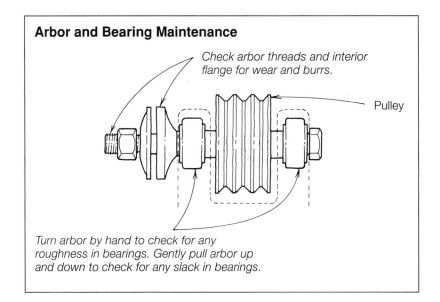

Arbor and Bearing Maintenance

Check arbor threads and interior flange for wear and burrs.

Pulley

Turn arbor by hand to check for any roughness in bearings. Gently pull arbor up and down to check for any slack in bearings.

Measure blade runout with a dial indicator.

blades. If the flange needs truing, remove the arbor assembly and take it to a machine shop. On older saws I have seen woodworkers take a sharpening stone to the arbor flange to get it 90° to the arbor.

You should also check for any runout on the blade itself. Blade runout can increase the amount of feed pressure needed and cause rough cuts. Even new blades have some runout, and they will develop more runout from slow feed rates, pinched stock, kickback and binding. Use a dial indicator against the blade body as you rotate the blade. If runout varies all around, the cause is probably a warped blade. The older the blade, the more runout. If extremes are 180° apart, the cause is more likely to be runout in the arbor flange.

V-belts and pulleys

Most modern table saws are driven from a motor via one or more V-belts, which convey the motor's torque to the arbor through the inside walls of the pulley. V-belts are made of an outside protective covering, a rubber body, and interior cording that is strong enough to resist stretching and carry the load. Since the sides of the belt need to make maximum contact with the pulley's inside walls, it is important that the V-belt be matched correctly and seated in the pulley so it comes nearly level with the top rim. A belt that is too wide will ride above the rim, causing some loss of power. A belt that is narrow or worn will bottom out in the pulley's landing, reducing contact with the sides and causing slippage to occur. The ensuing friction and heat will cause excessive wear to both the pulley and the belt.

Since using the correct size belt is so important, you should replace worn belts with new ones from the saw's manufacturer, or at least to the manufacturer's specifications. Never try to fit a new belt to a badly worn pulley; replace the pulley instead.

If the V-belts fit the pulleys correctly, the weight of the motor provides enough tension to transmit power from the motor to the saw arbor and to keep the belt from slipping. If your saw uses more than one belt, replace them all as a set, even if only one is worn; otherwise more of the load will be carried by the new belt or belts. Uneven loading results in premature wear and vibration in the saw. Vibration transmitted to the blade accounts for rough cutting even with the best of blades. Frayed belts will also cause vibration and should be replaced. I save used belts to use as spares singly or as a set for temporary emergency use.

Pulley/shaft alignment

The arbor and motor shafts should be parallel to each other, and the pulleys must be in alignment (see the drawing on the facing page). Even a slight misalignment will cause excessive belt and pulley wear from poor tracking, and also increase vibration and noise.

Since the arbor pulley is usually set in a designated position close to the arbor bearing, the adjustment is made by moving the motor and pulley. To make this alignment, loosen the setscrew in the pulley on the motor shaft. Place a straightedge on the arbor pulley so that it makes contact with both edges of the rim and then move the motor pulley until the straightedge touches both sides of its rim too.

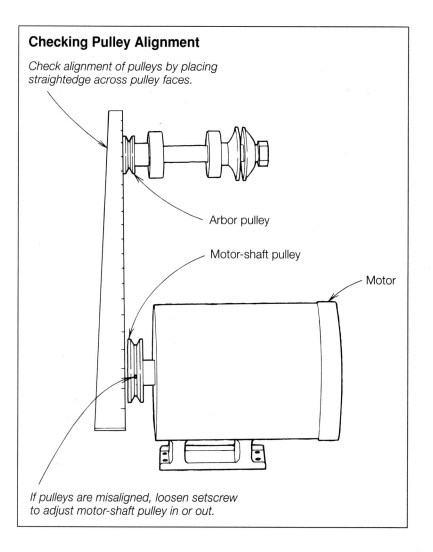

Checking Pulley Alignment

Check alignment of pulleys by placing straightedge across pulley faces.

Arbor pulley

Motor-shaft pulley

Motor

If pulleys are misaligned, loosen setscrew to adjust motor-shaft pulley in or out.

If the pulleys are aligned, then the shafts will be in line too. If you can't get the pulleys to align, it's because the shafts are not in line. In that case, loosen the motor mounts and shift the motor until you get the desired results. If the motor is slipping you should use lock washers on the motor bolts. The motor bracket should also be checked to see if it is worn or bent.

When you make this adjustment, it's best to get the pulley as close as possible to the motor bearing. A pulley at the end of a shaft puts unnecessary strain on both the shaft and the bearings. On contractor's saws, sometimes the guard that covers the belt and pulley will require adjustment after the motor pulley has been moved.

Cleaning and lubrication

Cleanliness and lubrication are essential for the smooth and accurate operation of your table saw. I've never gotten organized enough to set a schedule for lubrication and maintenance, but rather I tend to the internal parts when I notice some stiffness in the adjusting mechanisms and the external parts (such as the table, miter gauge and rip fence) when I encounter resistance. This generally works out to about once or twice a year for the internals and three to four times a year for the external working surface, assemblies and accessories.

Starting with the external surfaces, the saw table should be cleaned with mineral spirits and steel wool. It's important to keep the table free of moisture (don't set drinks or leave green wood on it), which can leave permanent marks in the steel. To remove rust or stains, use 400 to 500 wet/dry paper instead of steel wool. Metal polish and coarse automobile rubbing compound also do a good job of rust and stain removal.

Since most saw-table tops are made of cast iron, a fairly porous metal, waxing can really help in making a slick surface, which reduces friction between the table and the workpiece. For wax, I use up what remains in cans of furniture paste wax. Most car and floor waxes work equally well, but you should avoid products that contain silicone, which can contaminate the finishing process. Also avoid floor waxes that contain anti-slip additives and car waxes that contain abrasives.

To apply the wax, rub it into the table top, forcing it into the pores of the metal over the entire surface and miter-gauge slots. Apply just enough wax to coat the surface and allow it to dry before rubbing out. The table-saw frame and accessories — guide rails, extension tables, miter gauges and rip fences — will also benefit from an occasional coating of paste wax. Before waxing any assembly or surface, always clean it thoroughly of old lubricants, pitch, gum and packed sawdust. Use mineral spirits and steel wool on metal surfaces, and a damp cloth on any plastic parts.

Waxing makes for smooth, responsive working parts and helps resist moisture. It also makes the saw safer to operate. Waxed surfaces will not interfere with gluing or wood finishing as long as the excess is removed and the wax is buffed and dry. If a small amount is transferred to the workpiece, normal sanding will remove it.

Clean the interior of your saw frequently to prevent the accumulation of chips and sawdust, which can seriously impair saw performance. Pay particular attention to sawdust packed around the motor and the blade-height and blade-angle mechanisms. Cleaning is a good time to check the assemblies for excessive wear or damage, especially the worm gear and rack on the two shafts. If these are worn excessively or if teeth are missing, the gears can be replaced.

Most newer saws and motors are built with permanently sealed bearings, but if yours has lubrication fittings on the motor or arbor assemblies then give each a small a squirt of light machine oil at least twice a year. Don't over-oil, and don't oil anything that does not have an oil fitting. Oil on an exposed part of the saw will soon collect sawdust, which congeals into a gummy substance that gathers in and around the working parts, making them hard to operate and posing a possible safety hazard. Rubber drive belts will also deteriorate if they come into contact with oil.

The best lubricant for most moving parts of the saw is one that does not pick up a lot of sawdust, such as powdered graphite, hard wax or white lithium spray. Silicone and graphite will cause problems with finish adhesion if they come in contact with your wood, so they are best carefully confined to the internals.

Lubricate the worm gear and rack for both the tilting and height adjustment assemblies; if you use wax there's no need to buff it off. To lubricate the entire trunnion assembly begin with the trunnions set at 90° and then move them to 45°. The only other interior assemblies that may need lubrication are the two adjusting rods where they enter the cabinet and where their stop collars ride against the rack assemblies. In both places the stop collars can be loosened, slid back on the rod, cleaned, waxed and then returned to their original positions.

CHAPTER 5
Safety

According to a 1983 survey of *Fine Woodworking* readers, more than half of all the accidents that happen in the woodshop involve the table saw. Given the risks and the severity of the injuries, you might think that safety would be a top priority among table-saw users. Yet safety means different things to different people. Many woodworkers maintain that the best safety device is on their shoulders. A typical comment is: "I am careful and I have a safe attitude, but I don't use guards and safety accessories and I still have all my fingers." Does that make sense? Reasons given for not using safety devices are familiar and predictable: guards, splitters and other accessories get in the way, and they are too much trouble to use.

These excuses have an element of truth to them but they don't address the issue. Having worked with table saws for more than 20 years, I know both directly and indirectly of their hazards. I also know how easy it is to take precautions that will all but guarantee that you will not get hurt at the saw.

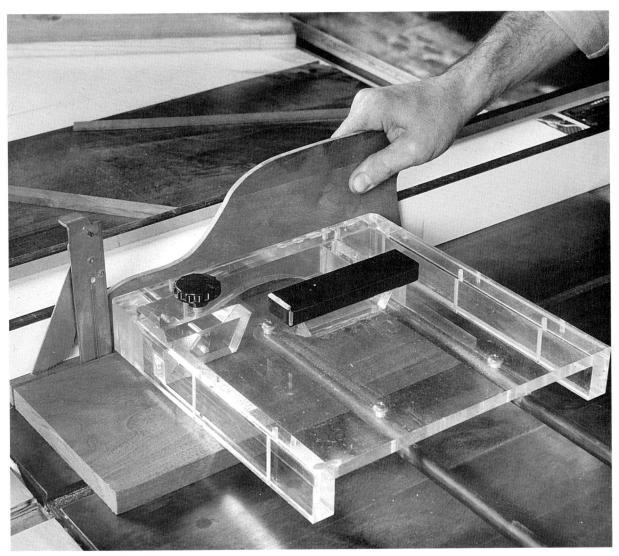

A blade guard and a splitter are essential table-saw safety accessories; using a pusher to feed the wood keeps your hand out of harm's way.

Kickback

The most common cause of table-saw accidents is kickback. Kickback occurs if the workpiece is suddenly grabbed by the sawteeth and hurled back at the operator. The operator can get seriously hurt or even killed by a flying piece of wood, but more commonly the hand guiding the workpiece finds its way into the blade. Anything that allows the teeth at the back of the blade to grab the wood can cause kickback, including problems inherent in the workpiece, an improperly set rip fence and pushing the wood through the blade in an unsafe manner. These problems can all be minimized by using a splitter on the table saw.

Common Causes of Kickback

Imperfect workpiece

Ripping improperly dried stock can cause saw kerf to spread open or pinch closed, leading to kickback.

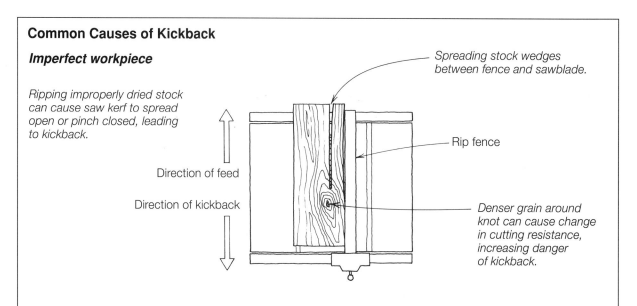

Spreading stock wedges between fence and sawblade.

Direction of feed

Direction of kickback

Rip fence

Denser grain around knot can cause change in cutting resistance, increasing danger of kickback.

Improperly set fence

If rip fence is angled toward blade, workpiece is guided onto back of blade. Lifting action of rotating blade can throw workpiece.

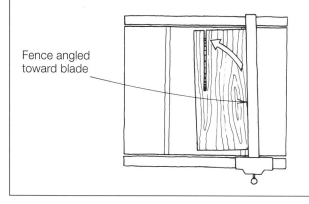

Fence angled toward blade

Incorrect pushing

Pushing forward too close to fence will direct workpiece to back of blade, causing kickback.

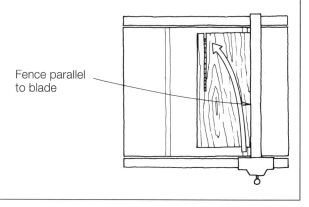

Fence parallel to blade

Imperfect workpiece

The ideal material for machining doesn't split, check, bow, twist or expand and contract in response to shifts of temperature or humidity. This ideal material never has knots or splits. Furthermore, it's of uniform moisture content throughout – it doesn't contain 10% moisture on the outside of the piece and 40% on the inside. Unfortunately, this ideal material isn't wood at all – it's medium density fiberboard (MDF), and I don't use it to build fine furniture.

What I do use are hardwoods, chiefly American hardwoods, and in Berea, Kentucky, that means cherry, walnut, oak, poplar, ash and maple. Like most species, these woods are prone to irregularities and flaws that can lead to kickback on the table saw. In my career as a woodworker I have encountered just about every flaw that occurs in wood, including nails and bullets.

Natural flaws   Knots are one of the more common natural flaws. It's safe to saw through tight knots, but loose knots should be removed or avoided because they may fly out of the workpiece. Crotch wood (found where branches enter the main trunk) can also be a problem because of interlocking grain. Figured wood can be fairly unpredictable in behavior. Pitch pockets – solid resin or empty voids within a piece of wood – may or may not present a danger to the woodworker who is sawing them, but the resinous material is hard on the sawblade.

Be cautious when defects such as checks, knots and splits approach the blade. The area around knots is much denser grain and can cause a sudden change in the cutting resistance. Cutting close to checks and splits will often produce a loose wedge that will fall in between the blade and the kerf, locking the two up.

Be sensitive to resistance in the wood. The more resistance, the more you have to push, and the more danger of kickback. If the resistance suddenly lessens, your hand may be carried right into the sawblade.

Drying defects   A number of problems can arise when wood is improperly dried. Case hardening occurs when the interior of the piece of wood retains high amounts of water while the surfaces are dry; in severe cases, honeycombing, or interior checks, may result. Case hardening is usually caused by kiln-drying too quickly. Reverse case-hardening occurs when the inside of the wood is drier than the outside. Both of these conditions give rise to stresses in the wood, which might not be apparent until you cut into the workpiece.

Severe cupping, twist, kink and bow are also the result of poor drying and storage practices. Twist occurs when the four corners of one face of the workpiece are not in the same plane. Cup is a deviation in flatness across the width of the board. Kink is a localized abrupt deviation from flatness or straightness, usually around knots or caused by misplaced stickers. Bow is a deviation from flatness in the length. Warped or twisted stock can grab and bind the blade.

Ripping stock that has internal drying stresses can cause the saw kerf to act unpredictably—it may either spread open or close. If it spreads open, the workpiece will wedge itself between the fence and the sawblade, and the blade, spinning forward, will tend to throw the work. One way to deal with a spreading kerf is to use a short rip fence, or half-fence, that extends only a short distance beyond the cutting edge of the blade (see pp. 95-97). If your saw is not equipped with a half-fence, anti-kickback fingers will help to prevent kickback. A splitter (see pp. 74-76) also helps by denying the workpiece access to the rear teeth of the sawblade, where more of its throwing force could be applied to the stock.

Table-saw safety guidelines

There's no magic formula for safety at the table saw. Many of the guidelines are the same as for operating any other machine. Concentrate on what you are doing, and don't look around or talk while operating the saw. Be aware that many accidents happen right after a large lunch, when you're usually less alert.

When planning your sequence of work, try to find the simplest way to set up a cut. A fussy setup can lead to problems. Let common sense be your guide—if something seems dangerous, it probably is. Take your time; rushing is an all-too-common cause of accidents in the shop.

And don't be a know-it-all. Overconfidence ("it won't happen to me") can lead you into taking potentially disastrous risks.

Dress
Anything that flaps around is potentially hazardous to the table-saw operator. That includes long hair that isn't tied back, necklaces, bracelets, ties and loose clothing. Don't work with your shirt pockets crammed with objects; pencils and rulers have a way of dropping onto or around the sawblade. Never wear sandals; your feet should be fully protected in a pair of good walking shoes or sneakers (good arch support and a nonskid sole are important features to look for). And don't wear gloves while you work; they easily catch on things and make your hands less sensitive.

Saw setup
The table saw is mostly metal, and should be plugged into a grounded electrical outlet. Never operate your saw in wet areas. When you are changing blades or doing routine tune-ups, always unplug the saw. Make all adjustments with the blade at a dead stop (and the saw unplugged). Set the blade no more than $\frac{1}{8}$ in. to $\frac{1}{4}$ in. above the workpiece; the higher the blade, the riskier the cut. Before ripping, make sure the rip fence is locked.

Hands and blade
If you keep your hands away from the blade, you reduce dramatically the likelihood of a serious accident. Some woodworkers like to mark the danger zone around the blade by painting a red stripe in the cutting area. Don't reach over

If the stresses caused by improper drying cause the saw kerf to close up, the workpiece will pinch the spinning blade, causing the blade to try and throw the workpiece. Unfortunately, the more you resist, the more off balance you become, and the more vulnerable you are to kickback if it occurs. Again the splitter helps by keeping the kerf from closing all the way where the full force of the turning blade would fight the piece off.

Even when using a splitter, a board with a lot of internal stress can clamp onto the blade and splitter like a starving dog on a juicy bone. The splitter does prevent the wood from being thrown, but it may not want to go forward either. It is best to turn off the saw as soon as you meet strong resistance and force the kerf open with a wooden wedge.

the blade or pick up cut stock until the blade comes to a complete stop (this is where an outfeed table really helps). Never attempt to clear scraps while the blade is turning.

Most table-saw accidents happen while ripping (see the discussion of kickback in the sidebar on p. 95). When ripping stock, use a pusher and make sure you have a solid cut end to push on. An end that is split, knotty, wedge shaped or irregular in any way is difficult to guide safely with a pusher.

Rip fence/miter gauge
Use the rip fence to rip and the miter gauge to crosscut — never cut freehand under any circumstances! Make sure that the miter gauge slides freely in its slot. Never use the rip fence as a guide with the miter gauge;

doing so will cause the wood to be pinched between the blade and the fence, resulting in kickback.

Cutting
Sharp sawblades are less likely to kick back. When you turn on the saw, allow the sawblade to reach full speed before cutting. Push the work all the way past the blade; stopping in mid-cut invites kickback. Most important, stand to the side of the workpiece being cut, not in line with it. If kickback occurs, the wood will travel in a line straight back from the sawblade. You don't want to be in that path.

Cleanliness
Order and cleanliness around the saw are essential to safety. Keep your saw table free of tools, scrap and extra workpieces. If they are left on the table, they

will eventually find their way to the blade; if they are metal, the blade could shatter. Using your hands to wipe sawdust off the saw table is a bad habit to develop, even when the blade is not running. Use a dust brush instead.

Keep your sawblades clean. Resin-covered blades build up heat and make it harder to push the stock through the cut, thereby increasing the risk of kickback. Finally, wash up after using the table saw to minimize skin problems if you are cutting particularly irritating woods. Protective creams applied to exposed areas of the body before cutting also help.

Improperly set rip fence

Any time that the workpiece laps over the cutting line of the rear teeth of the blade there is a real danger of kickback (if you don't use a splitter on your saw). That can happen when the rip fence is angled toward the rear of the blade, even a minute amount. The rip fence must be parallel to the blade or angled slightly away (see pp. 92-94).

Unsafe pushing

If the workpiece is pushed incorrectly during a ripping cut, it can drift away from the rip fence onto the back of the blade, leading to kickback. When ripping stock it's important to direct the workpiece toward the fence as well as forward and down. If you push forward only on the fence side of the sawblade, the workpiece will be directed toward the back of the blade.

Always continue pushing until the work is cut all the way through. Letting go of the work too soon is very dangerous. It may sound dumb, but I have seen it happen. A pusher that effectively directs pushing force toward the fence and holds the work securely to the table while elevating your hand well away from the blade is a necessity. (For more on pushers see pp. 81-82.)

Safety accessories

Besides the standard safety equipment that comes with the saw, there are many accessories that make the table saw safer to operate. These include splitters, blade guards, featherboards, safety wheels, pushers, power feeders and outfeed supports.

Splitters

A splitter (also called a riving knife or spreader) does just what its name implies: it keeps the saw kerf open. Ideally the splitter should be thinner than the saw kerf but thicker than the body of the sawblade. It should be positioned as close to the sawblade as possible.

In preventing kickback, the splitter is the first line of defense. The splitter prevents the wood from closing on or pinching the blade. More important, the splitter keeps the work from riding up on the back teeth of the blade, the inception point of kickback. This means that the work can't be thrown back at you!

There are several different splitter designs (the standard splitter is shown in the photos on pp. 13-14). The best splitter that I have used follows the curvature of the blade and can be adjusted so that it sits just below the top of the sawblade (see the photo at left on the facing page). Because of its curvature, it leaves only a small space (less than

The curved Inca splitter can be positioned right behind the sawblade, making it just about impossible for the rear teeth to grab the workpiece and kick it back toward the operator.

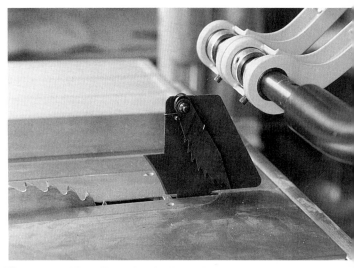

The removable splitter for the Delta Deluxe Uniguard comes equipped with anti-kickback fingers.

⅛ in.) behind the blade, so it's virtually impossible for the rear teeth to grab the work. This splitter is bolted to the saw carriage and moves with the blade (I call this a rising and falling splitter). Except when using a dado or molding head of a smaller diameter than your regular blade (where it isn't needed anyway), it stays out of the way. It doesn't need to be removed (as do most other splitters) for many different joinery cuts or slotting.

Unfortunately, most American-made table saws are not designed for the rising and falling splitter. There is no place on the arbor assembly to accommodate one. I hope this problem will be addressed when companies update their antiquated designs. Meanwhile, some manufacturers are at least considering the splitter problem. Delta now offers two splitters—one removable (see the photo at right above) and one that disappears under the throat plate (see the photo at right). Neither rises or falls with the blade, but they are an improvement on standard splitter designs.

After-market guard manufacturers are not required to supply a splitter or anti-kickback fingers with their guards. I found that both Delta splitters are fairly suitable companions to these guards, at least on Delta table saws. The disappearing splitter comes standard with the Delta Uniguard (see p. 79), and the removable splitter with the Delta Deluxe Uniguard. Both can be ordered separately from Delta to fit on Delta saws. I particularly like the disappearing splitter because it's there when you need it but can be pushed down under the throat plate

Delta's disappearing splitter and anti-kickback fingers can be pushed down under the throat plate when not needed.

when there are operations where it would be in the way. This kind of convenience makes for a safety device that you will automatically get used to using.

Anti-kickback fingers are the second line of defense in preventing kickback. They are usually attached to the splitter (less commonly, to the guard) and cannot be bought as a separate unit. For more on anti-kickback fingers, see p. 14.

Blade guards

A lot of woodworkers have no time for blade guards and even look down on those who use them, but I have learned to appreciate these essential safety devices. Blade guards help reduce the anxiety and tension of using a machine that can remove your fingers in an instant.

Whenever I use the table saw without a guard, I am on edge about what the blade might do, where to put my fingers, and how to hold the workpiece. I also have to squint my eyes in the flying sawdust, and the noise adds to the tension. The addition of a good blade guard almost immediately causes a lot of this tension to dissipate. That doesn't mean you don't have to be cautious while using the saw, but you have less to worry about, which enables you to give more attention where it belongs—to the job of making accurate cuts for your project.

Blade guards are standard equipment on all new table saws (see the photos on pp. 13-14), but these guards often leave a lot to be desired in terms of ease of use, visibility and ability to cover different tasks at the saw. These deficiencies leave the guards only minimally acceptable. It seems to me that table-saw manufacturers could come up with more creative solutions.

In spite of their drawbacks, the standard guard systems do provide adequate safety for the occasional woodworker, especially in most ripping and crosscutting operations. They are certainly much better than no guard at all, considering the severity of the possible injuries without a guard. Of all table-saw accidents reported, OSHA has recorded none where the guard and splitter were in place. The serious craftsperson really has no excuse for not investing in or devising safety devices that will keep body parts intact.

Replacement guards

As more people become aware of the need for table-saw safety, better safety accessories are becoming available. These include after-market replacement guards, four common makes of which are discussed on pp. 77-79 (for addresses of suppliers, see the Sources of Supply on pp. 174-176). Replacement guards generally offer better visibility of

Replacement blade guards are generally better designed and more convenient to use than the standard guards that come with the table saw.

The Brett-Guard

The Brett-Guard, manufactured by HTC Products, Inc., was the first guard that I tried after operating the table saw for about eight years without a guard. I have been very pleased with it and even though the Brett-Guard doesn't work in all situations, it is well on the way to working like a piece of safety equipment should.

The guard consists of a heavy-duty 11-in. square plastic box suspended on two round metal rods. The base unit is locked into a platform that you attach to either side of your saw on the extension wings. This setup requires drilling two holes for each platform. There is also a base plate for the back of the saw for covering long crosscuts up to 1 ft. wide.

What I like about the Brett-Guard is its excellent visibility. I like a clear view of the work, especially when cutting off just a little bit or when approaching a knot or other defect. The guard is easily removed and reattached, and it can be slid out of the way for blade setups.

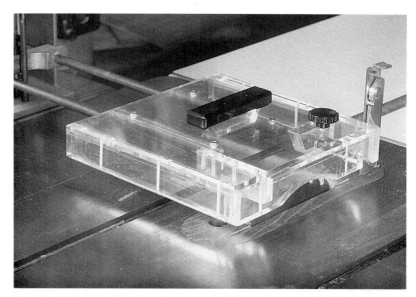

The Brett-Guard allows a clear view of the workpiece. Its height is adjustable, and it can be positioned close to the rip fence, allowing very narrow workpieces to be cut safely.

An adjustment crank on top of the base unit raises and lowers the plastic shield. The guard is meant to ride lightly on the work being cut, so it needs to be readjusted for different thicknesses. Since the guard stays suspended, you can adjust it to hover above the blade almost right up to the rip fence for cutting very narrow work (see pp. 110-111), a task that can't be done the same way with a conventional guard. The Brett-Guard can also be used to steady stock against the fence that is being cut on edge, as in edge grooving (see pp. 150-151).

Because the unit attaches to the sides of the saw you are limited to the capacity on that side when working with wide work. (HTC also makes a 50-in. suspended model for use with an extension table or a stand.)

The Brett-Guard doesn't have a splitter, though there is a small piece of spring-loaded metal that is supposed to prevent kickback. It works only when the guard is to the left of the saw, and I found that it didn't do much there except make scratches in the workpiece.

As nice as this guard is, I wouldn't use it (or any guard) without the addition of a workable splitter. You can use the Delta disappearing splitter (see p. 75), as I do, or you can make a good splitter from a small piece of Plexiglas, wood or metal attached to a slot in the throat plate. When you do this it's necessary to secure the throat plate in the opening so that it can't be lifted in the event of kickback. You can secure the

The Biesemeyer BladeGuard attaches at the end of the extension table to the right of the saw and enables you to rip and crosscut wide workpieces safely.

throat plate either by tapping for metal screws or by screwing on a small latch under the rear of the insert.

The BladeGuard

Biesemeyer's BladeGuard, which I have also used for a few years, is attached at the end of the extension table to the right of the saw. Between this guard and the Brett I am able to keep just about all my work covered. The BladeGuard is suspended on a 50-in. arm, made from 2-in. square tubular steel, that allows for panels to be cut up to that length without interference. There is no limit to the cutting capacity to the left of the blade.

Biesemeyer also makes a floor model of the same guard for those who don't have the extension setup. The company will also sell any combinations of the guard's parts, as I discovered when I was thinking about suspending the guard from the ceiling.

The BladeGuard provides good visibility, and I like the way that it lifts up and locks about 8 in. above the table so that I have easy access to the sawblade. The arm telescopes by means of a small crank at the end of the unit for adjusting the guard to one side of the blade or the other. This adjustment is important because with about 2½ in. between the inside walls of the guard there is a chance

that the guard might hold small cutoffs between the walls and the blade, resulting in kickback. Positioning the guard closer to the blade eliminates the problem.

Unfortunately, the 2½ in. allowed for using the guard with the blade tilted is not quite enough. With the blade tilted at the 45° limit there is very little space left, and with a 10-in. blade raised above 1¾ in. the blade can cut into the plastic sides of the guard, as I found out from experience. (Biesemeyer sent me a new side at no cost.)

The guard also comes with a battery-powered alarm that will sound when the guard is not being used. This feature might be handy for a school or an employee-training situation but I've never hooked mine up (I hate things that take batteries).

The guard can be moved away from the blade for those operations where it would be in the way, such as for cutting joinery into wide boards on edge or tall stock on end. At first, I found it tedious to take the time to turn the close-threaded rod the amount required to move the guard assembly out of the way and then back into place, so I adapted a socket to fit my cordless drill and speed-cranked the guard assembly with it. This arrangement helped somewhat but still wasn't ideal. Then I made two refinements that made the guard much more pleasing and therefore more likely for me to use.

First, I removed the rod and crank assembly altogether. This allowed me to slide the tube in and out of place with a minimum of effort. I can adjust it quickly where I want it without leaving the front of the table saw. A knob on top of the tube locks the setting in place so it can't move on its own. Second, I removed the wiring for the alarm that went through the tube into the blade cover, so I could easily pull the blade-cover assembly from its holder. Even though you can move the guard to the right, it only goes about 8 in. and can still interfere with some cutting operations.

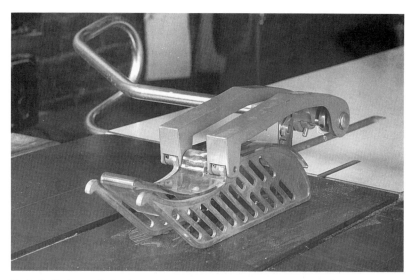

Delta's Uniguard, designed for the Unisaw, comes with an effective splitter and anti-kickback protection.

The Uniguard

Delta's Uniguard has some nice features and comes with a very good splitter and anti-kickback setup. This guard is on a tubular arm that mounts to the left rear of the saw. It allows a cutting capacity of 25 in. to the left of the blade and no limit to the right. (The Deluxe Uniguard now available has a 50-in. cutting capacity.)

The blade cover can be lifted and will stay out of the way while you make adjustments around the blade. The sides of the blade cover also lift independently of each other — a handy feature for rabbet cuts. The adjustable width also allows cuts to be made with the blade at full height at 45°. The whole unit was designed to be swung out of the way for long crosscuts to the left of the blade. You need to consider this in terms of your outfeed support, which can interfere with the swinging guard. The Uniguard can also be used in combination with HTC's fold-down extension rollers.

The Excalibur Overarm Sawblade Cover

Excalibur makes a suspended basket guard very similar to Biesemeyer's BladeGuard. The basket is a little wider and the arm can be adjusted by means of four wing nuts on the upright post. The tube is hollow to the blade cover for hooking up to a dust collector.

In commercial settings or where the table saw is in a permanent location it is not too difficult to adapt Excalibur guards to be hung from the ceiling. That way stock of any dimension can be cut without interference.

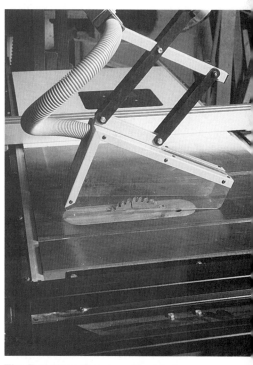

The Excalibur Overarm Sawblade Cover is a suspended basket guard with a 50-in. cutting capacity to the right of the blade.

the work, they are easily taken off or moved out of the way and re-placed, and they can be used in some cutting operations that can't be attempted with a standard guard. Because they are convenient, re-placement guards are more likely to be used.

Featherboards and safety wheels

Featherboards and safety wheels are shopmade or commercial hold-down devices that prevent kickback by holding the work firmly against the table and fence, allowing you to keep your hands farther from the blade.

Featherboards, or fingerboards, are wood, metal or plastic accessories that clamp in the miter-gauge slot or to the table and prevent the work-piece from moving backwards from the sawblade toward the opera-tor. Safety wheels consist of a pair of wheels that mount directly on the rip fence or, more commonly, on an auxiliary wood fence attached to the rip fence.

Safety wheels are sold commercially for saws that don't already have a good splitter, anti-kickback fingers and guard setup. The wheels adjust for various thicknesses of material and when properly set hold the workpiece firmly against the table and the fence. The wheels' one-way bearing allows the work to be fed through, but grips it tightly if there is kickback.

Safety wheels help prevent kickback by forcing the workpiece against the saw table and fence. Leichtung's Anti-Kickback Hold-Down Guide System, shown here, mounts on an auxiliary wood fence attached to the saw's standard rip fence. (Photo by Charley Robinson.)

Clamping a featherboard to the table guides the workpiece against the fence and allows the work to move only forward, through the cut.

Most woodworkers I've talked to who use safety wheels find them most beneficial for cutting sheet goods or large panels and when working from the side of the saw to cut grooves and rabbets. They are especially helpful in holding awkward work down and to the fence.

Safety wheels seem to be a popular substitute for a missing guard assembly, but I find them somewhat obstructive. Some require that you have to walk to the back of the saw and pull the board through in order to finish the cut, or use a push stick to push the piece under the wheels. Of course with a guard, splitter and anti-kickback fingers in place the wheels are not necessary for most cutting operations.

Pushers

Pushers are made of wood or plastic and are used as extensions of your hands to push the work through the sawblade. They are an important piece of safety equipment in that they take the chance of getting near the blade instead of your fingers. A well-designed pusher will also give you better control of the workpiece.

Pushers and push sticks are easily made in the shop out of plywood or solid-wood scrap. Their design can be adapted to suit the shape of the workpiece.

A shoe pusher feeds the workpiece through a narrow ripping cut.

Like many other table-saw accessories, pushers can be purchased or shopmade. Pushers can be made in many shapes, sizes and styles. My ideal pusher is one that keeps your hand well above the fence, allows you to exert pressure over a long distance of the wood being cut, feels comfortable to handle with no sharp edges, and is made of wood.

The pushers that I like and use the most are shaped like a shoe. I prefer these to what I call push sticks. A push stick doesn't hold the work down on the table as well, and you usually need two, one in each hand, to guide the work against the fence and through the blade. The shoe pusher is good for holding short pieces and does a good job of pushing thin and narrow work.

Shoe pushers have a long sole, a toe and a heel. I bandsaw my pushers freehand from scrap wood, making them tall enough to keep my hand above the fence. The long sole holds the work to the table and, in combination with the heel, against the fence. For the thinner pushers, I use plywood. The length and height of the toe can be varied to negotiate tight places, as when ripping very narrow stock and getting under the anti-kickback fingers. The thickness of the pusher should be proportional to the width of the workpiece. The heel also varies according to the thickness of the stock. My pushers range from $\frac{1}{8}$ in. to 2 in. thick — I use a $\frac{3}{4}$-in. thick pusher the most.

Power feeders

For production table-saw use, a power feeder may be a good option. Power feeders have a motor and wheels; they attach to the saw and feed the work automatically into the sawblade. Power feeders all but take away the danger of ripping since your hands are nowhere near the blade. They range in price from about $350 to over $1,500.

Outfeed supports

An important safety addition that is commonly overlooked is the back extension support. I would definitely urge you to add this support to your table saw, whatever the space confinements of your shop.

If the saw lacks outfeed support, many accidents can occur even when you're using guards. Look at your saw. You will notice that the surface area behind the blade is minimal. Even the shortest pieces of wood will fall off the table when you let go of them after they are cut through. If you don't want them to fall on the floor, you have to reach over the blade with one hand to retrieve the piece — a dangerous move, even with a guard. By extending the back of the table out, even 18 in., you will make operating the saw a lot safer and easier. With the work supported after the cut, you needn't be concerned with having to hold it down on the table (which becomes more of a task as the length of the work increases) or bringing it back over the blade before the blade stops running. (For more on outfeed supports, see pp. 41-42.)

Ear protection

The table saw is a noisy machine, and prolonged exposure to high noise levels can subtly but permanently damage your hearing. Noise is measured on the decibel (dB) scale, which is logarithmic; an increase of 10 decibels (say, from 90 dB to 100 dB) means that the noise is 10 times as intense. A normal conversation is about 60 dB to 70 dB; hearing loss begins with prolonged exposure at about 85 dB.

The table saw typically operates at about 100 dB. It also produces very high-frequency (pitched) noise, which is more likely to cause hearing damage. According to a report by the National Institute of Occupational Safety and Health (NIOSH), nearly 25% of woodshop workers have suffered permanent damage to their hearing from exposure to noisy machinery. Since hearing damage is so common, it's a good idea to have a hearing exam periodically to keep tabs on your hearing health.

Fortunately, hearing loss is preventable, and hearing protectors are the main line of defense. When you select hearing protectors, check their noise reduction rating (NRR), the amount of noise in decibels that they block out. Acceptable hearing protectors for the table saw

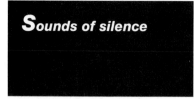

At a recent Health Fair, I found that I had a mild hearing loss at high frequencies, which is unfortunately most noticeable at conversation level. It is also permanent. I was surprised at first, since I have been faithfully wearing hearing protectors in the shop for the last seven years. But I hadn't used them for thirteen years before that, and hearing loss comes from accumulative exposure to noise over a period of time.

Noise is not something that you notice as you are working. On the contrary, the more you use the table saw without hearing protectors, the more you get used to it. You get used to it on two levels — you are accustomed to hearing it, and your hearing is physically deadened.

The opposite is also true. The more you use hearing protectors, the less tolerance you have for noise. Now I'll put them on when I use any power tool in the shop, even the bandsaw, which is not usually considered loud. I even got an extra pair to wear at home while mowing, chainsawing (up to 130 dB) and weed eating. I am thankful that, except for natural aging, my hearing is not getting worse.

should have an NRR of at least 25. Even though hearing protectors reduce the noise to your ears, you can still hear ordinary conversation with them on.

Safety gear is worthless if inconvenience deters you from using it. The hearing protectors that are comfortable and handy to put on are the ones you are most likely to use. There are three types of hearing protectors — hearing bands, ear muffs and ear inserts. Of these, the first two are the ones I use regularly in my shop.

Hearing bands

Hearing bands, my favorite form of ear protection, are lightweight plastic bands that fit either under the chin or behind the head. They have plastic or foam ear pads at their ends that fit into or over the ear canal. Because they come in bright colors, hearing bands are easy to locate, and they fit around your neck loosely so they are right at hand without being a nuisance. Hearing bands don't weigh much (less than one-third of an ounce), and they can be worn for long periods without much discomfort.

I prefer hearing bands with the softer foam pads to the plastic cone type. The cones are made to fit different-size ear canals, but I find that after a short time they feel as though they are painfully enlarging my canals. Also, the plastic feels like plastic. The plastic cones can be cleaned, while the foam pads come with replacements (extra pads can be ordered from the supplier).

I bought my first pair of hearing bands through a woodworking catalog and then saw the same pair from a safety supplier for one-quarter the price I paid. Hearing bands are inexpensive enough (a pair costs $4 to $6) to allow you to experiment to find the right type for you.

Ear muffs

I also use full-sized ear muffs to protect my ears from machine noise. The first ear muffs I had, which I bought at the local hardware store, were heavy and uncomfortable. I wore them only at the thickness planer, the loudest machine in my shop.

The ear muffs I use now are much lighter and more comfortable, and I can wear them for longer periods. (They also keep my ears warm in winter in my cold shop.) The main reason that I don't use them as much as the hearing bands is that they feel as if they're choking me when I pull them down around my neck. And if I hang them up somewhere, they are sure to be on the opposite side of the shop when I need them next. If you really like ear muffs the best, however, there are simple belt loops available that you can hang them on.

With ear muffs, you have to be careful that glasses or safety spectacles don't break the seal around the ears. Any air that gets to the ear canal will carry sound and reduce the effectiveness of the protectors.

Ear inserts

Ear inserts are small cylinders, typically made of foam, that expand inside the ear canal to block out noise. They are inexpensive and comfortable to wear, but my hands are invariably too dusty to use them.

Dust protection

The table saw doesn't put out the dust that sanding does, but given the frequency of its use it does enough to cause some real hazards. The federal Office of Safety and Health Administration (OSHA) has determined that exposure to airborne wood dust from western red cedar in excess of 2.5 milligrams per cubic meter of air (mg/m^3) and to dust from any other hardwoods in excess of 5 mg/m^3 is hazardous to health. This is a very, very small amount of dust.

Exposure to dust from wood and composition materials has been associated with skin and eye irritation, allergic reactions, asthma, nasal cancer, Hodgkin's disease, colon cancer, rectal cancer and salivary-gland cancer. Wood dusts have not been proven to be a direct cause of cancer, but it doesn't take a sleuth to figure out that they aren't good for you. The dusts of certain woods may be especially irritating or allergenic to susceptible individuals, and those woods should be avoided. That's why I never use western red cedar, some mahoganies and sassafras, and I almost never work with exotic species.

Wood dust does not have to be noticeably irritating to be doing damage to your system. It can be hazardous in other ways too. At the table saw, a steady stream of fine dust and chips is shot from the sawblade tips and gullets toward the operator. What doesn't get thrown is distributed within the saw and cabinet or below on the floor. The floor in front of a busy table saw can get covered with sawdust very fast. Sawdust is slippery, and especially dangerous when ripping, an operation that calls for some foot movement. (A nonskid safety mat at the front of the saw helps.)

Dust reduction at the table saw

There are a number of ways to reduce your intake of sawdust. For one, keep your sawblades sharp — sharp blades will make shavings while dull blades make dust. Sharp blades are also safer to operate and give you better results. A second way to cut down on the amount of dust in the air is to use a blade guard. A guard placed over and around the sawblade will deflect a lot of the debris back through the table insert or onto the table, not right toward you. A guard not only helps to keep sawdust out of your lungs but also out of your eyes, skin and other parts of your body.

Third, you can keep both your shop and lungs much cleaner by installing a dust-collection system, as outlined on pp. 37-40. Some of the smaller saws have bags below the arbor assembly, while most can be hooked up to a dust collector.

Finally, you can cut down on some of the sawdust by not using the saw! You can make many cuts with a handsaw. With a good bowsaw you can cut a board to rough length more quickly than making a setup at the table saw. I'm not saying that you should do most of your sawing by hand but rather not to depend on the machine for all your cutting tasks. I have always felt that it is good not to get too far away from the material that you are working with, and sawing by hand will keep some of your other fine motor skills sharp.

Using some kind of a dust mask will keep harmful particles out of your lungs. Shown here are a disposable two-strap face mask and a half-mask with replaceable filters.

Dust masks

Over the years, I have tried a number of dust masks and always been unhappy with them. Discomfort, poor fit, difficulty in breathing, and fogged-up glasses are a few of my gripes. Recently, however, I have found two types of mask that I can tolerate: a soft silicone half-mask and a two-strap face mask.

The soft silicone half-mask fits tightly over the face, and has a breathing valve and replaceable filters for dust. Half-masks are safety approved by NIOSH, and they can also be fitted with organic-vapor filters for protection against the chemicals in wood finishes and strippers. I use these dust masks for prolonged sanding and exposure to dust.

Two-strap face masks are approved for lower concentrations of dust. They are disposable and cost less than $1 each. I use these masks for short bouts with sawdust and to outfit occasional helpers. Two-strap face masks should not be confused with the more common one-strap masks, which are not safety approved. I find these thinner masks to be awkward fitting, because they make it difficult to get a good seal. Also, my glasses fog up when I use them.

Eye safety

In my early days as a woodworker, eye protection was not a safety area that greatly concerned me. I wore regular prescription glasses and felt that they provided adequate eye protection for all my work at the table saw. In addition, I was (and still am) diligent in using blade guards and a dust collector, which greatly reduce the amount of particles that come flying off the saw. What's more, the safety glasses and goggles that I'd tried were a hassle to use, and the hassle didn't seem worth it.

Over the years, however, I have come to learn that regular prescription glasses are not designed to withstand heavy impact, and even with guards and dust collectors in place you are still susceptible to eye injuries. These injuries range from a trivial speck of sawdust in the eye to serious puncture wounds that require immediate medical attention (see the sidebar on the facing page). I am now a firm believer that some form of eye protection is essential for the table-saw operator.

Safety eyewear is now available in much greater variety than it was 20 years ago. There are glasses with designer-style frames, adjustable temple lengths and tinted lenses. With accessories like ear pads, elastic holders and safety cords, safety glasses are comfortable to wear. They are also relatively cheap — from $2 to $8 (suppliers of safety

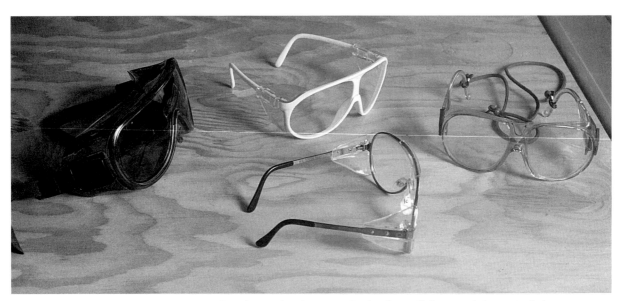

Goggles and safety spectacles keep flying particles out of the eyes. They should always be worn when operating the table saw.

Eye injuries in the woodshop range from irritating to painful to sight threatening, and it's important to know how to deal with them. The most common injuries involve small particles in the eye. Very small particles of sawdust are normally flushed out naturally with an increased flow of tears; if not, they can be removed by flushing the eye with clean water with the eyelids apart.

Many times a small particle that is stuck under the upper eyelid can be removed by pulling the upper lid down over the lower lid. The eyelashes of the lower lid will wipe the inner surface of the upper lid and usually remove the particle. You can also grasp the eyelashes of the upper lid and turn the lid over a cotton swab. The particle can then be removed with a piece of sterile gauze.

Particles can be removed from the lower lid by pulling the lid down and exposing the inner surface. Again, the corner of a piece of sterile gauze can be used to remove the piece. Obviously you need to be very gentle when trying to remove a particle from the eye. You should never use a sharp object, such as a sharpened piece of wood or the point of a knife. And try to resist the natural urge to rub the eye — you can cause scratches of the eye tissue or actually push the splinter into the tissue.

A particle can scratch the eyeball, and even if the piece is removed it may feel like something is still in there. If this feeling persists you should seek medical attention. It is quite possible for a piece to be in the eye yet not be visible. Small pine slivers, for example, can become almost clear with the addition of water from your eyes. These and other small pieces can be made visible with a dye administered by a medical professional.

If you're not wearing safety eyewear or using a blade guard, small chips flying from the saw at 100 mph can stick in the eye or, worse, puncture it. If a particle stays lodged in the eye swelling and infection may occur, but you shouldn't try to remove it yourself. Instead, cover the eye with a bandage compress and have someone take you to a doctor. If you're alone don't hesitate to call an ambulance.

If you get hit in the eye by a piece of wood, a cold compress will alleviate the pain and swelling. If you feel pain inside the eye or experience blurred or double vision, get medical help as soon as possible. Blood under the cornea of the eye is usually a sign of a cut eye. Don't rub the eye — putting pressure on a cut eye can force the inner fluid along with the retina out of the cut, and partial to total blindness can occur. The procedure for a cut eye is to place a sterile bandage over the eye and then protect the eye from pressure with a piece of cardboard or similar material. Again, call an ambulance if you are alone.

With any eye injury that you are not sure how to treat, it is better to go to a doctor immediately than risk discomfort or possible loss of sight.

equipment are listed in the Sources of Supply on pp. 174-176). The eyewear options available include safety spectacles, scratch-resistant safety prescription glasses, and goggles.

Safety spectacles

Safety spectacles approved by ANSI (American National Standards Institute) are anti-fog, anti-static and anti-scratch. They are moderately impact resistant but not unbreakable. If there is danger of severe impact, it's a good idea to wear a face shield in addition to safety eyewear.

Safety prescription glasses

I have been using scratch-resistant safety lenses in my glasses for quite a while (contact lens won't work in a dusty shop environment). This type of lens is available for regular, bifocal or multifocal (progressive) lenses. When you order safety prescription lenses you must specify polycarbonate for high-impact resistance. Safety lenses aren't as good as safety glasses because they lack top and side shields, but frames are available that have protection above and either permanent or replaceable side shields.

Goggles

Goggles have given me the eye protection that I need when doing tasks at the saw that produce more dust than the guard and collector can handle, such as cove cutting (see pp. 117-119) and finger jointing (see pp. 167-170). Cutting coves at the table saw makes very fine dust that will fog the shop, and when cutting finger joints the cutoff fragments come up the standing workpiece right into your face.

Even though these operations (and machine sanding) are bothersome, for years I wouldn't wear the hardware-store goggles I owned. They were soon so scratched and uncomfortable that I felt they were worse than the dust. I depended on fans to blow the dust outside in the summer or somewhere else in the shop during cold weather. Today, much better quality goggles are available, and I have a good comfortable pair that is anti-fog and scratch resistant.

First-aid procedures

Woodworkers should become familiar with basic first-aid procedures for removing splinters, dealing with eye injuries (see the sidebar on p. 89) and controlling bleeding. The best way to become familiar with these procedures is to add a first-aid guide to your shop library. Standard references include *The AMA Handbook of First Aid and Emergency Care* (Random House, 1990) and *First Aid Guide* (National Safety Council, 1991).

It's also very important to know what to do in the event of severe hand lacerations or amputated fingers, which, unfortunately, are not uncommon occurrences at the table saw. I asked a local hand surgeon for a list of recommended procedures for dealing with serious hand injuries, and I strongly advise that you do the same.

Every shop should have a first-aid kit and a fire extinguisher.

A basic first-aid kit for the workshop should include:

- sharp tweezers
- scissors
- adhesive tape
- 2x2 and 3x3 sterile pads
- 1x3 sterile bandages
- adhesive bandages
- antiseptic wipes
- antiseptic ointment
- instant cold compress
- mild pain reliever
- plastic gloves

Every workshop should have a well-equipped first-aid kit in a convenient (and known) location. A fire extinguisher is another essential piece of safety equipment. Keep the phone numbers of your doctor, nearest hospital and ambulance service in plain view at the telephone and make sure you are familiar with the route to the hospital. If you have a programmable telephone, one-button emergency dialing can save your life.

CHAPTER 6
Ripping

Ripping and crosscutting, the two basic table-saw operations, are fundamentally different tasks. Ripping is cutting with the grain of the wood (along the length of the board); crosscutting, which is discussed in Chapter 7, is cutting across the grain of the wood. Ripping to rough width is usually the first table-saw operation performed on a piece of wood. The board is fed, end first, through the blade, with the long edge of the board guided by the rip fence.

Before a board is ripped, one face needs to be flat, so it won't rack into the blade and possibly bind. One edge also needs to be straight and usually at 90° to the face; this edge will ride against the rip fence. Preparing the face and edge is called "surfacing" the wood (see the sidebar on p. 94).

The rip fence

Every table saw comes with a rip fence (see pp. 8-9), which must be properly aligned for the blade to cut safely and efficiently. As discussed on p. 56, the rip fence can be set parallel to the sawblade, or slightly out of parallel (with the fence a mere $\frac{1}{64}$ in. farther from the rear of the sawblade than from the front of the blade). If the fence is set exactly parallel to the blade, your cut will be fairly smooth, but the

Ripping a board to width is a basic table-saw operation.

Wood to be cut on the table saw needs to have at least one face and one edge that are flat, straight and at right angles to each other. The straight edge rides against the rip fence, while the flat face lies flat on the saw table. A board that is distorted is more likely to bind between the blade and the fence, producing kickback and putting your hands in danger of being cut.

The first edge and face of the workpiece are most commonly surfaced on a jointer. The opposite face is usually established with a thickness planer. If you do not have a machine to prepare the wood, you can buy it surfaced from most suppliers. Hand planing is another option, but it becomes very time-consuming on large projects.

Once your wood is prepared, it's a good idea to rough-cut the pieces for your project to approximate dimension as soon as possible. The longer the wood sits, the more likely it is to distort. Similarly, after final dimensioning, cut the joints and assemble the work as soon as possible.

rear teeth of the blade will be needlessly cutting after the front teeth have done their work. There will be more resistance in the cutting action, too.

With the fence angled slightly away from the blade, the cut will be very clean and there will be less resistance while feeding the stock. You can definitely feel when the fence is set right. But caution is in order: If the rip fence is set too far away from the rear of the sawblade, the workpiece will crawl away from the fence, creating a tapered cut, and burn on the waste side of the cut.

Occasionally (as in bevel ripping on some saws), you may need to move the fence to the other side of the blade, so if your fence is angled slightly out, you will have to reset it when you move it. In this case the fence can usually be adjusted by hand-tightening, then nudging and measuring. The benefits gained from angling the fence are well worth the readjustment for the few times that the fence is used on the opposite side of the blade.

Never allow the rip fence to angle toward the rear of the sawblade. This configuration will cause the workpiece to bind and burn, or worse, the workpiece may be grabbed by the rear teeth and flung back at you in a dangerous kickback (see the sidebar on the facing page).

On many table saws, the standard rip fence leaves a lot to be desired in terms of accuracy, cutting capacity and locking parallel to the blade. These limitations can be overcome in various ways. Many woodworkers like to attach a board, or auxiliary fence, to the standard fence. Another type of fence, more common on European table saws, is the half-fence, which makes it impossible for the wood to bind against the back edge of the sawblade. A third solution to rip-fence shortcomings is to replace the standard rip fence with one of the several replacement rip-fence systems available.

Auxiliary fences

An auxiliary fence is a board, usually plywood or a dimensionally stable hardwood, that is attached by bolts through holes in the rip fence (see the drawing on the facing page). The auxiliary fence allows the fence to be moved very close to the blade without the danger of cutting into the metal on the rip fence. An auxiliary fence can also be used to even out any imperfections in the metal fence, such as a bow. Add paper shims between the auxiliary fence and the rip fence to square the fence to the table. If you make an auxiliary fence, remember to cut a 1/8-in. by 1/8-in. rabbet along the bottom edge as an escape for wood chips and sawdust that might otherwise keep your work from riding against the fence.

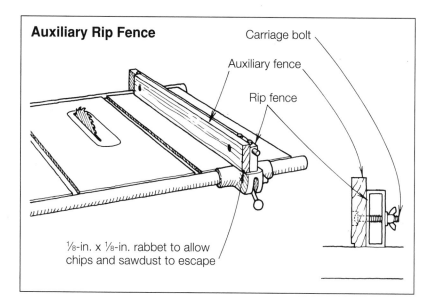

Auxiliary Rip Fence

Carriage bolt

Auxiliary fence

Rip fence

⅛-in. x ⅛-in. rabbet to allow
chips and sawdust to escape

Even when the fence-to-blade setting is perfect, kickback can occur if the workpiece comes in contact with the rear teeth of the blade, which is possible if there is no splitter on the saw. It takes very little drifting away from the fence for the work to start lapping over the cutting line of the rear teeth. Pushing the workpiece forward into a spinning blade creates resistance, and the workpiece tends to rotate away from the fence and onto the back teeth. A widening kerf tends to wedge wood between the fence and the blade, while a closing kerf pinches the blade.

The two main lines of defense against kickback are the splitter (see pp. 74-76) and anti-kickback fingers (see p. 14). The splitter prevents the wood from doing any more than rubbing on the side of the blade, which means that the work can't be thrown back at you. The anti-kickback fingers prevent the work from going backward toward the operator.

The most common types of auxiliary fence are the low fence, the high fence and the extended fence. A low fence is advantageous when trimming panels that have overlapping veneer or plastic laminate; it also allows for more hand space between the fence and blade when cutting narrow pieces (see p. 109). A high fence is used when standing work on edge, as for edge grooving for tongue and groove. An extended fence that reaches past the back of the table saw is useful when cutting sheet goods (see pp. 107-109).

Half-fences

Many European table saws incorporate a fence system that is shorter than the fences normally available on small American-made table saws. The half-fence, as it is called, extends only a short distance beyond the front gullets of the blade, thereby eliminating the risk of the wood binding against the fence at the back of the cut (see the photos on p. 96). A half-fence guides the wood into the cut but does not keep it pressed against the rear teeth of the blade, so the cut is smoother.

Safety is the major reason for using a half-fence. If the workpiece is drier on the outside than on the inside (a common situation), the saw kerf will tend to open wide, and a full fence would force the workpiece into the blade, causing burning and possible kickback. With a half-fence, the workpiece can expand unencumbered past the end of the fence.

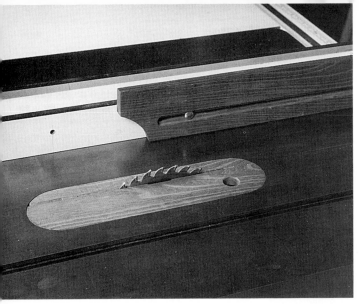
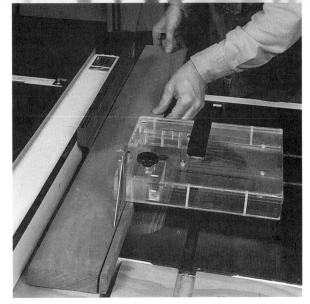

The half-fence, which extends just beyond the cutting edge of the sawblade, allows the workpiece to spread apart at the back of the cut without risk of kickback.

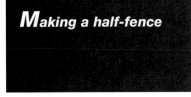

Making a half-fence

A half-fence is not difficult to make. Use a durable, stable material, such as maple or high-quality plywood. If you are handy with laminates, a laminated face will help stabilize the wood and make a slick surface for the workpiece to slide against. The fence should be taller then the largest sawblade your machine can handle and no more than 1 in. thick (thickness does not necessarily add stability and it reduces the cutting capacity of your saw). Like all fences, the half-fence should have a small rabbet at the bottom to keep sawdust and chips from holding the stock away from the fence. This rabbet is generally the same width as the sawblade (⅛ in.) and equal depth.

Make the half-fence long enough so that its front edge extends 1 in. past the gullets at the front of the blade. Since the position of the gullets varies with the height of the blade, the position of the fence should also change with each blade-height setting. The half-fence I made has a countersunk slot; by using two bolts and wing nuts it can be secured to a saw's standard or replacement fence. It is adjustable and easy to remove. However, a stationary fence set for the blade's lowest setting, usually to about 1 in. behind the arbor hole, will also work fine.

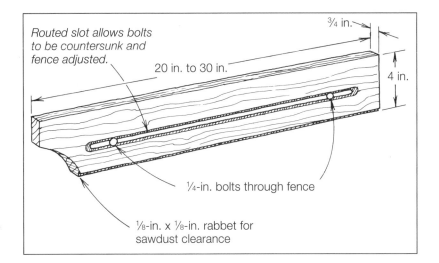

Routed slot allows bolts to be countersunk and fence adjusted.

¾ in.

20 in. to 30 in.

4 in.

¼-in. bolts through fence

⅛-in. x ⅛-in. rabbet for sawdust clearance

The best way to get a feel for how the half-fence works is to make one (see the sidebar on the facing page), set it up and try some rip cuts. You may feel a little insecure at first because the workpiece is not supported after the cut, but you will soon get used to working with the half-fence. With a long fence you worry about keeping the workpiece against the fence after the cut as well as before it, and you end up putting pressure against the work in the wrong place. With a half-fence you guide the work through the cut, applying pressure toward the fence only before the sawblade.

Is the half-fence a good idea? Opinions vary. I have used both systems for a number of years and find that there are advantages to each. I like to use a half-fence for ripping rough lumber, but a longer and sturdier fence is much better when cutting unwieldy sheet goods.

Replacement rip fences

If you spend a lot of time at the table saw, a replacement rip fence can make your work a lot more accurate, efficient, safe and enjoyable. Replacement rip fences are especially handy when used in conjunction with extension support tables for cutting sheet goods.

Setting up a standard table-saw rip fence for a precise cut is always a chore for me. It usually requires measuring and re-measuring with my folding rule at both ends of the blade for each new cut. This fussiness

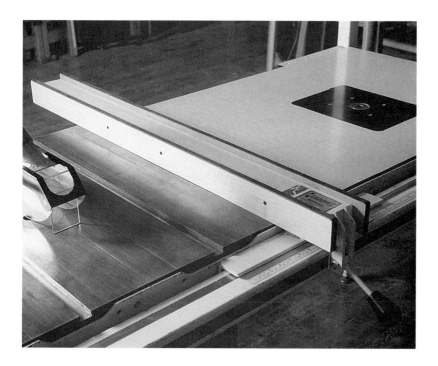

Replacement rip fences are superior to the standard rip fences that come with moderately priced table saws. This Biesemeyer fence locks perfectly parallel and as much as 54 in. to the right of the blade.

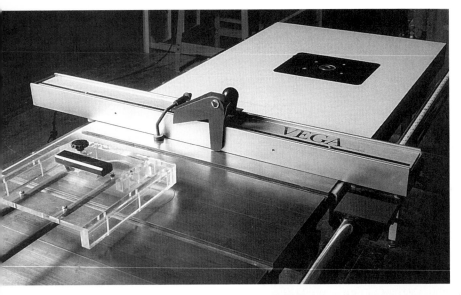

Other replacement-fence systems include the Vega fence (shown above with optional 'Finger Saver' accessory) and the Excalibur T-Slot fence (right).

in the standard rip fence has led to the development of more precise replacement-fence systems. After-market rip fences include Accu-fence, Biesemeyer, Excalibur, Jet Lock Fence, Paralok, Unifence and Vega (see Sources of Supply on pp. 174-176 for manufacturers' addresses). These fences fit all the popular saws; some systems require drilling holes in the saw because the rails don't always match up with the saw's existing holes. All replacement fences are reasonably easy to install in a few hours at most.

Replacement-fence systems have a much longer locking mechanism at the front of the fence and a reliable measuring scale — a built-in tape measure that allows accurate setting of the fence without tedious measuring from the fence to the blade for every cut (see the photo below). The built-in measuring scale is a feature I really like. Being able to depend on a parallel fence and accuracy of the scale eliminates the need to measure to the blade, so your work will go more quickly and safely.

Replacement fences range in price from about $250 to $450; some are heavily discounted when purchased with a table saw. You can also make your own fence out of aluminum and steel channel for about $100. There are good plans for a shopmade fence in *Fine Woodworking* magazine *(FWW #68, pp. 46-47)*; using simple tools, it should take you about 20 hours to make.

Rails come in various lengths for each fence system. When moving up to a replacement rip fence it's a good idea to opt for rails that will allow at least 4-ft. ripping capacity to the right of the blade, which makes cutting sheet goods and other large work much more manageable.

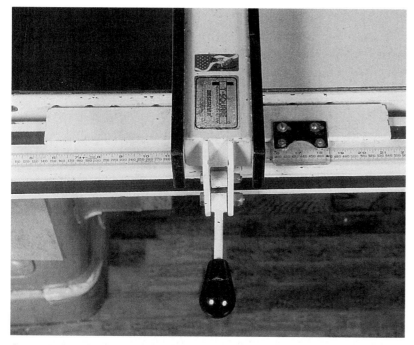

A convenient locking mechanism and built-in measuring scale are handy features of the Biesemeyer replacement rip fence.

Absolute accuracy is shooting
for a precise measurement. You
strive to set the rip fence to the
dimension indicated on your
plan. However, in most
woodworking, the fit is what is
important in the end, even if the
measurement is not the correct
one. Instead of figuring out the
width of some pieces
mathematically or measuring
when duplicate parts are
needed, you can use the part
itself to set the fence distance.
This way of working is known as
relative accuracy.

I work to relative accuracy when
cutting out drawer fronts to their
finished width before milling the
sides. I use each front to set the
fence for the sides for that
drawer. Here a slight deviation in
size is not as noticeable as a
joint that doesn't fit.

Standard ripping

The general procedure for ripping a board involves setting the blade
height, setting the fence, and, with guards in place, making the cut.
Your stance at the saw is critical to accuracy and safety.

Setting the blade

Place the board to be cut next to the sawblade and raise the blade
about ⅛ in. above the wood. The higher the blade, the less resistance
in the cut and the cooler the blade runs; however, these advantages
must be weighed against the danger of having the blade more exposed
and the disadvantage of more tearout at the bottom of the cut. With a
sharp blade and a tuned saw the benefits of a high blade are minimal.
The best response I have heard on the question of how much the blade
should protrude above the work is, "How much do you want to cut into
your fingers?"

When making rip cuts, use a sawblade designed for ripping. (For a discussion of sawblade types, see pp. 24-26.) Rip blades cut like a chisel,
removing small chips from the cut. The blade I usually reach for when
doing a lot of ripping is an alternate-top-bevel (ATB) blade with 30 to
40 teeth. I prefer a thin-kerf blade. The difference in feed resistance is
noticeable, even with a 3-hp motor.

Setting the standard rip fence

Move the rip fence to the desired width, as shown in the photo at left
on the facing page. For an accurate cut with a steel blade, measure from
the fence to the point of a tooth on the front of the blade that is set toward the fence. (On a carbide blade the teeth have no set, so you can
measure to any tooth.) In certain situations, you can use an already-cut
piece to set the fence instead of measuring (see the sidebar at left).

If you were using a replacement rip fence with a dependable measuring scale, you would now be able to lock the fence in place. With a
standard rip fence, however, setting the fence is not so simple. When
you move the rip fence back and forth it drags on the back rail; since
the sleeve at the front is usually too short to prevent racking, the fence
will not consistently lock parallel to the blade, which is a potentially
dangerous situation.

For best results, move the fence toward the blade when resetting
rather than away from it. Push on the front sleeve of the rip fence directly in line with the fence body after the fence has been moved, then
lock the fence. This pushing action will help line up the fence at right
angles to the front rail. Double-check your setup by measuring from
the fence to the front and back of the sawblade. The feedback you get
from this information will let you know how your fence is working.

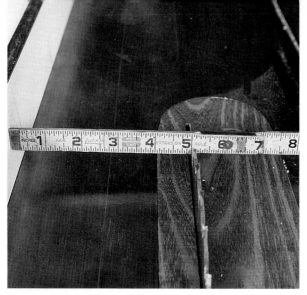

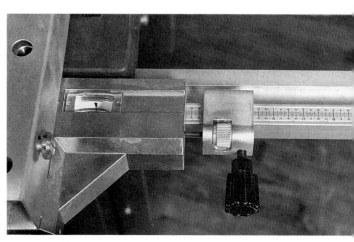

To set the rip fence, measure from a tooth set toward the fence if you are using a steel sawblade. With a carbide sawblade, measure from the inside edge of any tooth, as shown.

A micro-adjuster makes it easy to move the rip fence a hair in or out.

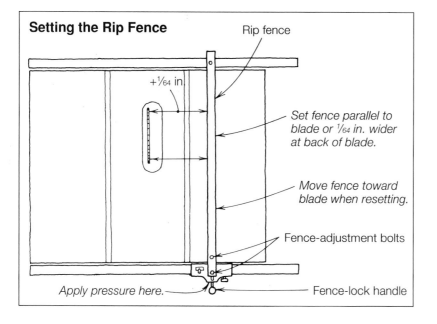

Setting the Rip Fence

Rip fence

+1/64 in.

Set fence parallel to blade or 1/64 in. wider at back of blade.

Move fence toward blade when resetting.

Fence-adjustment bolts

Apply pressure here.

Fence-lock handle

A micro-adjuster is a handy fence feature, but too often it is left off of fences or is not accurate enough to be a real help. Having to give the fence a little nudge to make the cut just right can get to be very frustrating. One way that I deal with this problem is to make a reference mark with a pencil on the saw table along the side of the fence before I move it.

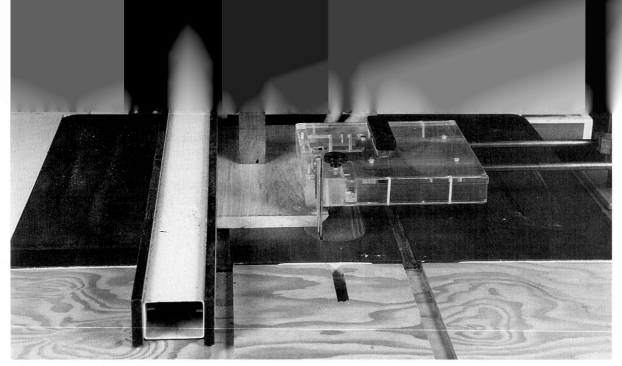

During a typical rip cut, a board's jointed face and edge are directed down toward the saw table and against the fence. The operator stands to the side of the board, and finishes the cut with a pusher.

Making the cut

Whenever possible, orient the workpiece with its finished or outside face up; since the blade cuts from top to bottom, any tearout will be on the bottom face. Place the guard over the blade and put on your safety gear. Make sure the saw table is free of debris before you turn on the machine.

With the workpiece pulled back, turn on the saw and allow the blade to reach full speed. Place the workpiece on the table with its straight edge against the fence and move the stock into the blade. Continue to feed the work at a steady rate, about as fast as the saw will cut (cutting speed is a function of the size of the saw). Feed rate is a matter of feel. Too slow a feed causes more friction and burns the edges of the work-piece. Too fast a feed jams the work into the sawblade, risking kick-back or an overheated motor. The sound of the saw will tell you if the motor is slowing down or the blade is meeting too much resistance.

Stance

The common tendency to stand back from the table saw while ripping is dangerous. The farther from the saw that you stand, the more you have to overreach while making a cut, which is not only awkward but also tends to throw you off balance.

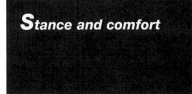

Stance and comfort

Standing to the side of the blade, out of the line of fire if kickback does occur, is essential for the safe operation of the table saw as well as for accurate cutting. If you stand to the side and feed the wood through the cut as described on p. 102, kickback should not be a problem.

My first full-time shop was in a barn with a concrete floor. It didn't take too many hours of standing to appreciate the relief that a rubber pad under my feet afforded. Even though I am fortunate enough to have wood floors now, I still use a rubber pad in front of the table saw (and other work stations around the shop). These pads greatly help reduce leg fatigue.

They also provide a nonslip area amidst the sawdust and shavings around the saw. (For a manufacturer of rubber fatigue pads, see the Sources of Supply on p. 174.)

Sometimes adjusting your vertical position at the saw can make you more comfortable. While cutting a number of finger-jointed boxes, I found that standing on a low frame with a piece of plywood tacked to it not only helped my legs but also raised me up to a much more comfortable position for this tedious operation.

Speaking of standing, a good pair of shoes goes a long way toward keeping your legs and feet from developing problems. Whenever you have to stand in one place for long periods, as at the table saw or workbench, worn-out or cheaply made shoes will wear on your feet, even if your shop has a wood floor.

Standing on a rubber mat at the saw helps reduce leg fatigue. Note also that the operator's left foot and hip are braced against the saw to help stabilize his body.

Stand at the front of the saw, to the left of the blade, with your left foot in contact with the base and your hip against the front rail. In this position the saw helps to stabilize your body, leaving your arms free to manipulate the work. Your right arm is in a straight line with the work being pushed along the right side of the sawblade. You are using your whole body to apply force in this cutting line. When the cut is complete you are in a comfortable balanced position.

It's a good idea to use a pusher as extra protection when rip cutting. I generally use a pusher for work that is less than 8 in. away from the sawblade. As an extension of my hand and arm I find the pusher gives me added control and an extra measure of safety. Pushers are discussed in detail on pp. 81-82.

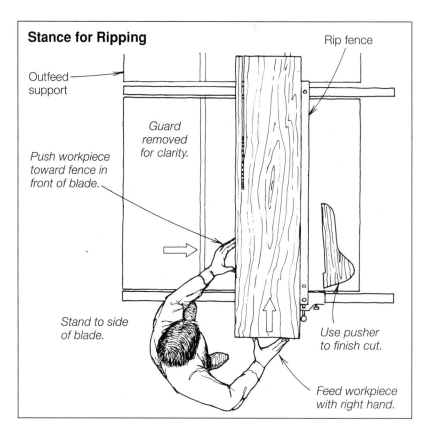

Stance for Ripping

Rip fence

Outfeed support

Guard removed for clarity.

Push workpiece toward fence in front of blade.

Stand to side of blade.

Use pusher to finish cut.

Feed workpiece with right hand.

While ripping, your attention should be on the workpiece where it makes contact along the fence, not at the sawblade. Make sure you keep the workpiece against the fence as you feed the work through the sawblade. With your left hand you can apply light pressure on the workpiece toward the fence before the blade, while the pusher in your right hand holds the work down and against the fence as the cut comes to the end.

Ripping long stock

Some form of outfeed support is necessary when ripping long boards. This support can take the form of a table or a helper. I usually use one or two support stands when cutting a long board, but when I have a number of boards to cut I get help if it is available.

Outfeed support stands can be freestanding or fixed, shopmade or store-bought. Freestanding adjustable stands are commonly available commercially, as are units that attach to the back of the saw; some fold down when not in use. (For more on outfeed supports, see pp. 41-42.)

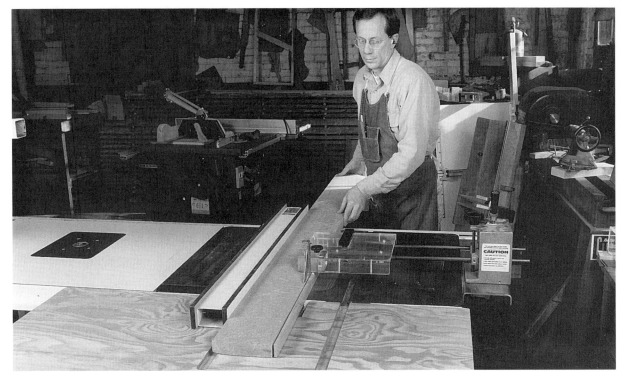

An outfeed support table is especially helpful for ripping long stock.

A helper, or "tail-off" person, who understands how a table saw operates can make cutting a long board safer. The helper is a human support stand who can also return the work to you. The helper should never pull on the board, because this tends to throw you off and it's impossible to pull in a straight line.

My son has learned to work with me well. He supports the board with both hands underneath and does not try to guide it in any direction. After the work has been cut he pushes the waste piece back to me, well away from the blade, and stacks the finished work. You soon work out a rhythm for accurate and safe cutting.

Whenever I rip or crosscut any work, but particularly a long board, I always prepare a straight edge and a flat face (see p. 94). My pusher is at the end of the saw table so that it will be there when I need it. The fence and blade height are set, and the splitter and guard are in place. The outfeed support is lined up to receive the cut pieces.

When you rip long boards, you start out away from the saw, with the back end of the board raised slightly, and end up at the saw (as for standard ripping).

At this point I prop the board at the front of the saw and turn on the machine. By the time the stock comes in contact with the blade, the piece should always be flat on the table. This is rarely a problem except on long boards, where the overhanging weight tends to make it difficult to keep the board level with the top. A good way to compensate is to lift the back end of the board higher so that the front end of the board is in firm contact with the table. Lifting the board also makes it easier to guide the edge against the fence.

As the stock size varies you'll start at different positions in relation to the saw but end up in the same position as always when you complete the cut. For long boards you start out away from and in front of the machine. Begin the cut by walking the board forward, holding it as you would a shorter board. With your right hand, feed the board in line with the fence. With your left hand as far as you can reach comfortably on the left side of the board, apply pressure diagonally to keep the edge of the board against the fence. Grab the pusher as soon as the end of the board reaches the saw table. As you complete the cut, you will end up against the body of the saw and to the left of the blade.

Ripping sheet stock

I don't use plywood or other man-made materials very much in my work as a furniture maker, but there are times when I need to rip sheet stock — for example, when I build jigs or do utility work around the shop. (We talk about "ripping" sheet stock if we are cutting it to width using the rip fence, even though it doesn't have a grain direction.)

Two major problems when cutting sheet stock are size and tearout. Most sheet stock is 4 ft. by 8 ft., and maneuvering such a large sheet across a small saw table can be unwieldy. As in ripping long stock, cutting sheet goods demands a helper or the use of extension supports, not only in the back but to either side of the table saw as well, especially if the material being cut is thin and floppy. These supports can be either freestanding or attached to the saw. They should be sturdy and even with the table surface.

An extended fence is also helpful when cutting sheet stock. Alternatively, you can clamp a long, straight-edged board under the stock and use it as a guide against the left edge of the saw table. This method is also handy when the edge of the material is not even (see pp. 114-115). Whatever fence you use, you may need to clamp it at the back of the saw table to resist the increased sideways pressure.

To help minimize tearout, use a throat plate with an opening the same size as the saw kerf that will give backing to the bottom of the cut. (For a discussion of shopmade throat plates, see the sidebar on p. 61.) Spe-

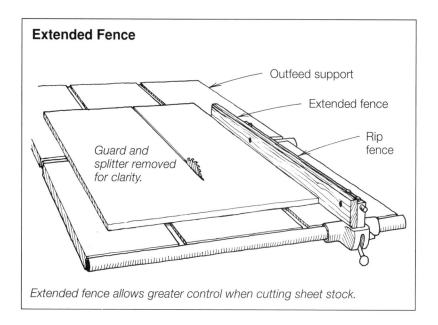

Extended Fence

Outfeed support

Extended fence

Rip fence

Guard and splitter removed for clarity.

Extended fence allows greater control when cutting sheet stock.

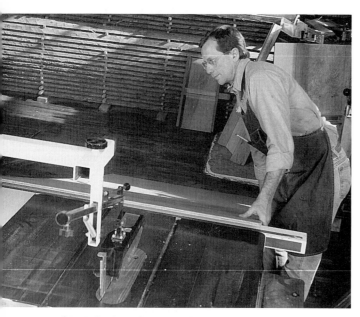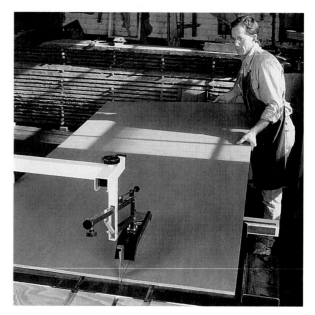

Start ripping sheet stock by bracing the sheet against the front of the saw table (above). Standing at the rear left corner of the sheet (above right), walk the piece forward while applying pressure into the fence in front of the blade (facing page, left). Move toward the fence as you approach the front of the saw and push the sheet forward with your right hand between the fence and the blade (facing page, right).

cial plywood-cutting sawblades with 60 or more teeth are available that will minimize splintering. Of course, if there is a good side to the work, place it face up.

If the work is fragile (a fine laminate, for example) and you are experiencing tearout at the bottom of the cut, try making a preliminary pass with the blade set for a very shallow scoring cut. This cut will slice the fibers clean, and there will be no tearout when the piece is cut through. The same trick will work for any crosscuts where you want to eliminate tearout.

Generally when cutting sheet stock you stand much farther to the left of the blade than when ripping solid wood. The best way to manipulate the panel is from the far left rear corner, where you can guide the piece in a straight line to the fence and push forward at the same time. Your left hand holds the left outside edge about 1 ft. from the corner, and your right hand is at arm's length at the rear.

Cut by walking the piece forward and maintain pressure with the fence right at the front of the blade. Do not apply sideways pressure on the material after the cut. As you approach the front of the saw, shift your body closer to the line of cut. Push along the alley between the blade and the fence with your right hand, and move your left hand closer to the corner, where pressure is still in line in front of the blade

against the fence. Your push stick can either be waiting on the sheet or at the saw within easy reach. Grab it and continue to push the sheet through the sawblade, as in ripping a long board.

Cutting a 4x8 sheet can be one of the more challenging table-saw operations, but as long as you have the correct supports and feed the material as described above, sheet material is not difficult to cut safely.

Ripping narrow stock

The challenge in cutting narrow stock is the fence's proximity to the blade and guard. Ripping very narrow stock will not allow the hand to pass safely between the blade and the fence. With a conventional guard, when the workpiece gets too narrow (less than 2 in. wide) the guard and splitter actually get in the way of the cutting operation.

Many woodworkers endanger themselves by removing the standard guard to rip narrow stock. However, there are a number of safe ways to rip narrow stock. If the piece you need is not too narrow (at least 2 in. wide), you can use a thin pusher and a low auxiliary fence (see the drawing at right), which allows more room for your hand between the guard and the fence.

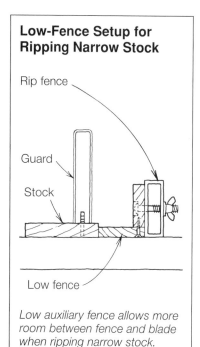

Low-Fence Setup for Ripping Narrow Stock

Rip fence

Guard

Stock

Low fence

Low auxiliary fence allows more room between fence and blade when ripping narrow stock.

Jig for Ripping Narrow Stock

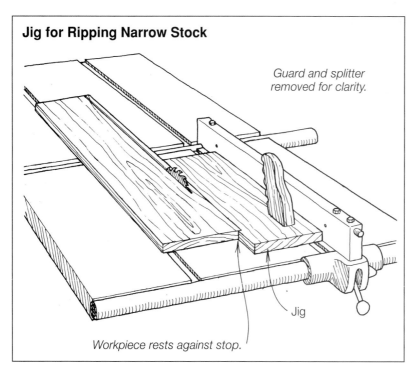

Guard and splitter removed for clarity.

Jig

Workpiece rests against stop.

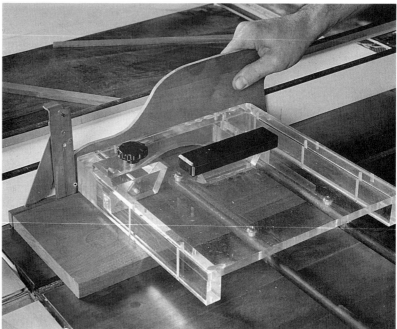

With a suspended guard over the blade and a thin pusher to guide the work, you can safely rip a very narrow piece.

If the piece you need to rip is narrower than 2 in., you can build a simple jig to guide the workpiece through the blade. This jig is nothing more than a piece of wood with a handle and a stop, which the workpiece rests against (see the drawing on the facing page). Hold the handle on the jig in your right hand and steady the corner of the workpiece with your left. If the stock is very narrow, use a push stick in your left hand to guide the board lightly against the jig. Keep the push stick in front of the blade to prevent the kerf from being pinched closed. With this jig you can cut pieces as thin as you like, as long as the throat-plate opening won't swallow them. (To make a replacement throat plate with an opening the same size as the saw kerf, see the sidebar on p. 61.)

A third alternative is to use a suspended guard such as the Brett-Guard (see pp. 77-78). Unlike standard basket guards, suspended guards cover the blade even when ripping very narrow stock. By using a pusher thinner than the distance between the blade and the fence, you can rip down to ⅛ in.

One final way to rip narrow stock is to move the fence over and cut the piece off the outside edge. This method works fine if you are just cutting one piece, but it's inefficient if you need several because you have to reset the fence for each cut.

Ripping short pieces

Ideally, you should always cut short pieces from longer, larger stock. However, it's not at all unusual to have short pieces of stock that will work for some of the smaller parts in a project, such as cubbyhole-drawer parts, knobs and short stretchers.

Trying to rip a short piece of wood between the fence and the blade is asking for trouble. Since the wood doesn't reach the splitter before it is cut through, it can very easily end up being thrown. The best and safest way that I have found to rip short pieces is to use a cutoff box that holds the work securely and takes it beyond the back of the blade; the process is described on p. 134.

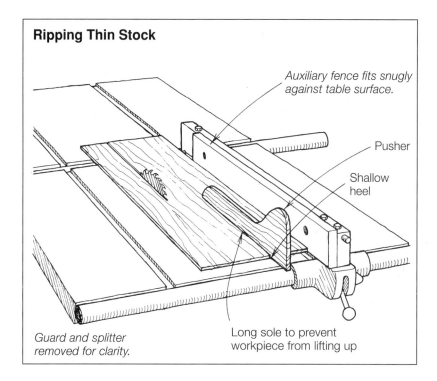

Ripping Thin Stock

Auxiliary fence fits snugly against table surface.

Pusher

Shallow heel

Guard and splitter removed for clarity.

Long sole to prevent workpiece from lifting up

Ripping thin stock

Ripping stock that is ⅛ in. thick or less requires a pusher with a shallow heel and a sole that is long enough to keep the piece from lifting up onto the blade as it is being cut. Some people use hold-downs (see pp. 80-81) to keep the stock from crawling up the blade, but I find that they get in the way. A good pusher can do the job safely. Outfeed supports also can help when cutting thin, floppy material. If you're working with an auxiliary fence, it should fit against the table surface to prevent the thin stock from sliding underneath it.

Ripping thick stock

The thicker the workpiece, the harder the saw has to work to cut through it. If the stock is thicker than the cutting capacity of the blade (see the photos on the facing page), the saw has to work even harder since the wood chips cannot be ejected and the blade runs hotter.

When cutting through thick stock, it is important to listen to the motor and adjust your feed rate accordingly. As in other ripping operations, go as fast as possible without bogging down the motor. If the resistance is high even though the blade is sharp, you might try a thinner blade. A thin-kerf blade is easier for the saw to push since it is removing less material in the kerf.

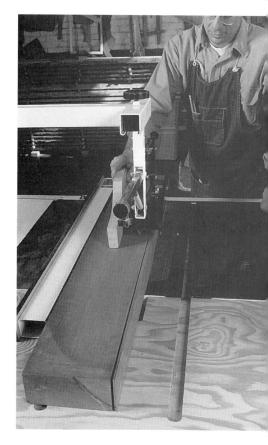

If your blade isn't big enough to rip thick stock in a single pass (top left), make one cut from one side (top right), then flip the board and complete the cut from the other side (above left and right). You have to remove the splitter for this cut because it's an incomplete cut, so be especially mindful of kickback.

It's not a good idea to rip thick material in a number of shallow passes. Thick material is more likely to distort, and you can end up with a piece that is no longer flat to the fence. Also, the quality of the cut will be poor. With stock that is too thick to cut in a single pass, make one cut from one side and then flip the board over to complete the cut, as shown in the photos above.

Resawing

Resawing is sawing a piece of wood on edge, usually down the center of its thickness, into two or more thinner pieces. Resawing is very dangerous on the table saw, especially if the on-edge workpiece is taller than the height of the blade. Having the blade buried causes a lot of heat, the standard guard can't be used, and balancing tall, narrow work without binding on the sawblade is difficult. Because of the dangers involved I strongly recommend resawing only at the bandsaw.

Ripping irregular stock

Sometimes it is necessary to cut a straight edge on a board that has two irregular edges. You encounter this situation with lumber that has been milled with the waney edges left on the board. With a bandsaw, you can cut a straight edge and even it up at the jointer. But the job can also be done at the table saw.

One way to rip irregular stock on the table saw is to attach a straight-edged guide board to the workpiece. First draw a straight line (the desired cut) to one side of the workpiece. Use a straightedge or snap a chalkline. Attach a thin, straight board (as shown in the drawing below) so that it overlaps the waney edge and is parallel to the first line. Use small finish nails or brads to attach the board to the waste portion. This guide board rides against the fence so that you can proceed as in a

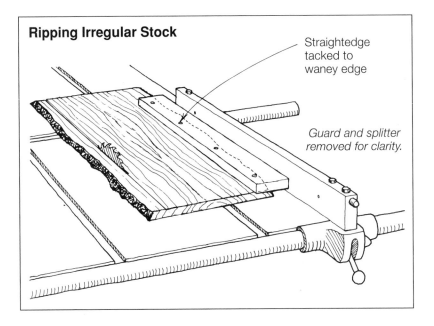

Ripping Irregular Stock

Straightedge tacked to waney edge

Guard and splitter removed for clarity.

One way to rip irregular stock on the table saw is to clamp the workpiece to a sled that has a straight edge, and guide the sled along the rip fence.

normal ripping cut. When the cut is complete, remove the guide board and use the straight edge you just cut against the fence to make your next ripping cut.

Another way to rip irregular stock is to use a sled that rides in the miter slot. Hold-downs attached to the sled secure the workpiece as it is being cut (see the photo above).

Ripping at an angle

There are times when you need to rip boards at an angle — that is, not parallel to the grain. For example, you may want the grain oriented in a particular way for either strength or appearance, you may have a bow or defect in a plank you want to avoid, or you may be able to get more width out of a board by ripping at an angle. Cutting tapered legs for furniture is a common application for the angled rip cut.

To rip a board at an angle, secure it with hold-downs in a sled that rides in the miter-gauge slot (see the photo at right) or against the rip fence. The hold-downs are adjustable across the sled's width, allowing you to hold work safely at almost any angle.

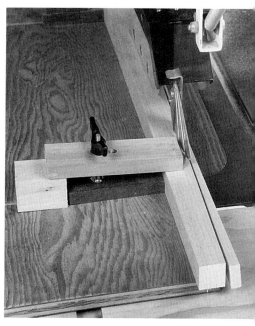

Tapers can be cut safely on the table saw using a sled with adjustable hold-downs.

Ripping an unsurfaced board

It's not always possible or desirable to joint and thickness-plane your stock before ripping. For example, if you try to remove a large cup at the jointer, a 1-in. thick board could be reduced to ½ in. or less, and the board could still cup again after it is finished. To be assured of getting the thickness you need when using cupped, twisted or warped boards, you might have to rip or cut them before preparing a flat face and edge.

The safest solution is to use a bandsaw to prepare the work before jointing, but unsurfaced boards can also be ripped on the table saw. First, cut the stock into the shortest lengths possible to minimize the problem. The question then arises whether to rip with the concave or convex side of the board on the table. Some woodworkers like the concave side up so that the flattest part of the board makes contact with the table at the blade. When the board is cut through, it is not apt to bind between the fence and blade. However, it is difficult to cut this way without rocking the workpiece.

I feel more confident ripping with the concave side down, because the workpiece is easier to manage during the cut. When the piece is cut through, it will drop and may wedge between the fence and the blade. Anti-kickback fingers are helpful here, as is a half-fence (see pp. 95-97). You can also rip warped, twisted and cupped boards using either of the setups described on pp. 114-115 for cutting waney edges.

Ripping bevels

Cutting a bevel with the grain is very similar to standard rip cutting except that the blade is tilted at an angle other than 90°. To avoid kickback and obtain a cleaner cut edge, be sure to angle the blade away from the fence and use a splitter.

On most table saws the blade tilts to the right, so you have to put the fence on the left side of the blade. Tilt the blade to the desired angle away from the fence and adjust its height, then align the fence for the desired width. Make the cut as with straight ripping.

Always cut bevels with the sawblade tilted away from the rip fence. The fence will usually have to be moved to the left of the blade.

Cutting coves

Coves are decorative cuts that I often use for molding and raised panels. They can be cut on the table saw by clamping an auxiliary fence to the table and feeding the workpiece into the sawblade at an angle. Cutting coves on the table saw is not strictly a ripping operation, but because it requires use of a fence it makes sense to discuss it here.

Begin by laying out the desired cut on the end of the workpiece that will come in contact with the blade first. Place the layout next to the blade, and raise the blade to the correct height. Use a stiff, fine-toothed blade. Smaller-diameter blades give a smaller curve, and tilting the blade makes the curve steeper.

Next, use an adjustable parallelogram jig (see the drawing below) to determine the angle for the auxiliary wood fence. Set the jig to the same width as the cove layout, then angle the jig until the far tooth of

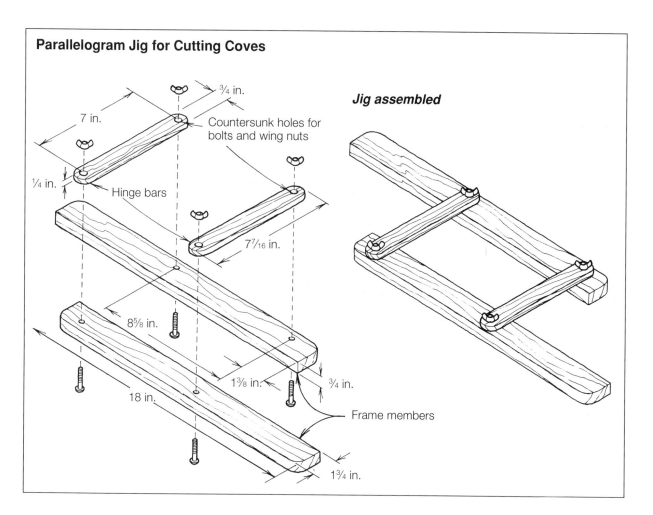

Parallelogram Jig for Cutting Coves

¾ in.

7 in.

Countersunk holes for bolts and wing nuts

¼ in.

Hinge bars

Jig assembled

$7\frac{7}{16}$ in.

$8\frac{5}{8}$ in.

$1\frac{3}{8}$ in.

¾ in.

18 in.

Frame members

$1\frac{3}{4}$ in.

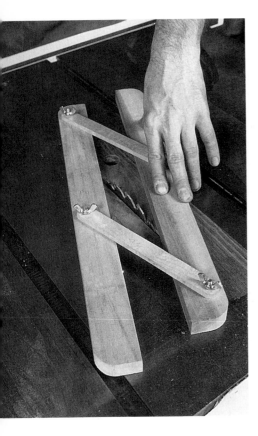

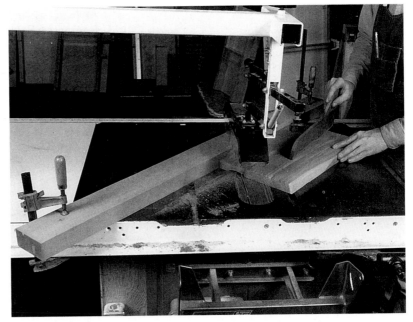

To cut coves on the table saw, use a parallelogram jig to determine the angle at which to set the auxiliary fence (left). Clamp the fence to the saw table and make a series of light passes obliquely across the sawblade (above right).

the blade just touches the left arm and the tooth closest to you meets the right arm (see the photo at left). Now clamp the auxiliary fence at this angle on the downward side of the blade. The fence itself is located so that the centerline of the work will intersect the centerline of the sawblade. (To cut a half cove on the edge of a board, the fence is moved forward so that it partially covers the blade, as shown in the photos on the facing page.) Because you will feed material at an angle, the fence will help keep the stock in contact with the blade.

Lower the blade to about ⅛ in. above the table. You'll need to take light cuts because there is a considerable amount of side stress against the saw. With the guard in place, position the material against the fence and start to feed the stock into the spinning blade. Use a shoe-style pusher (see p. 82) to guide the stock over the top of the blade. Never put your hands over the top of the blade.

Make repeated passes, raising the blade about 1/16 in. each pass. Make the last pass at full height. I sand out the rotary marks left by the sawblade using 100-grit sandpaper wrapped around a shopmade spindle on the lathe, but you can also sand by hand.

Cutting half a cove for a raised panel proceeds much like cutting a full cove, except that the sawblade is partially embedded in the fence.

CHAPTER 7

Crosscutting

Crosscutting is cutting wood to length across the grain. Work is generally crosscut after it has been ripped to width and the sides are parallel. The board is fed crosswise into the blade, guided by a miter gauge, sliding crosscut box or sliding table.

For the most part, crosscutting is a less dangerous operation than ripping. Since the workpiece is not confined between the blade and the fence, there is little danger of it kicking back. With miter-gauge cutting, it's the cutoff piece that is left near the blade and is prone to be thrown—the smaller the cutoff, the greater the risk. As with ripping, the splitter and the blade guard are important safeguards.

Miter gauge

The miter gauge is guided by a metal bar that slides in slots machined on either side of the sawblade and parallel to it (see pp. 9-10). The body of the gauge, which can be set to various angles from 30° to 90°, supports the workpiece as it is pushed through the cut.

One way to crosscut a board to width is to use an auxiliary fence
attached to the miter gauge.

For most crosscutting operations, I find the miter gauge, with its small body and single guide bar, inaccurate and awkward. Two ways to get around the shortcomings of the standard miter gauge are to add an auxiliary fence or use a replacement miter gauge.

Auxiliary fences

Adding an auxiliary fence to the body of your miter gauge will improve its performance somewhat. A simple auxiliary fence increases the bearing surface for the sides of the workpiece, stabilizing it during the cut. One common auxiliary-fence design is described in the sidebar below.

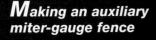

*M*aking an auxiliary miter-gauge fence

Make your auxiliary fence from stock ¾ in. thick and a little taller then the miter-gauge body. Length can vary with intended use, but 24 in. seems to work fine for most crosscutting operations. The board must be stable and have two parallel flat faces. Any fence works more efficiently with a clearance rabbet at its bottom. A ⅛-in. by ⅛-in. rabbet will help keep dust and chips from holding the work out from the fence.

Many woodworkers cement a piece of sandpaper to the working face of the auxiliary fence to help hold the workpiece steady. The extra grip is particularly handy when making miter cuts, which tend to push the piece away from the blade as it is being cut.

Screw the auxiliary fence to the miter gauge through the two predrilled holes in the miter-

gauge body. The fence should sit a paper's thickness above the table top, so it won't scrape as it moves (scraping the edge of the fence across the table sounds a lot like fingernails on a chalk board). For the initial cut the fence should extend past the

blade. Make the cut with the blade raised higher than the fence, to cut the fence even with the outside of the blade. For subsequent cuts you can use the end of the fence as a reference for the marked end of the workpiece.

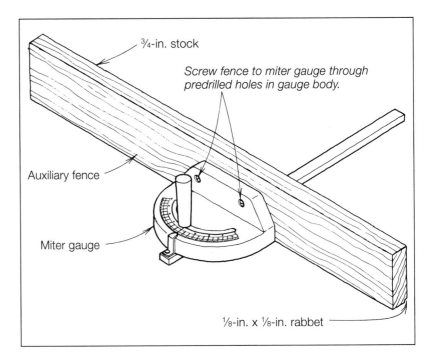

¾-in. stock

Screw fence to miter gauge through predrilled holes in gauge body.

Auxiliary fence

Miter gauge

⅛-in. x ⅛-in. rabbet

An auxiliary fence that extends past the sawblade will push cutoff pieces past the blade, where they can't be grabbed by the saw teeth and thrown back at the operator. Note the sandpaper attached to the face of the fence for added traction.

One safety problem with crosscutting on the table saw is that small cutoff pieces gather around the sawblade as you make repeat cuts. These pieces fly when they contact the blade. If the cutoffs are very small and narrow they can also slip into the opening in the throat plate. Many accidents happen when the plate lifts up or the small pieces become projectiles. For safer crosscutting, make an auxiliary fence that extends past the sawblade to support the cutoff pieces, as shown in the photo above. The fence has to be taller than the thickness of the workpiece; otherwise, the blade will cut it off. In use, the side of the fence that extends past the blade carries the cutoff pieces out of the danger zone. Set up an outfeed table to catch the pieces as they reach the end of the saw table.

Replacement miter gauges

The inadequacies of standard miter gauges have led to the development of a number of after-market replacement miter gauges. Most of these gauges, which range in price from about $50 to $150, have a long body to provide greater support for the workpiece. The backing fence is typically an aluminum extrusion, which is adjustable to give support right up to the blade at any angle. Some systems have adjustable drop stops that make setting up for repetitive crosscutting easier and more efficient (see the photos on p. 132). Many of the desirable features of replacement miter gauges are standard features on miter gauges on some European table saws.

Sliding crosscut box

The shortcomings of the miter gauge are especially apparent when crosscutting very long or very wide work. After struggling with large workpieces supported only by an auxiliary fence on a miter gauge, it slowly dawned on me that there had to be a better way to make accurate crosscuts. And so was born the first of my sliding crosscut boxes.

The sliding crosscut box consists of a flat plywood base, which is screwed to two hardwood runners that slide in the miter-gauge slots. The workpiece sits on the base and is fed through the sawblade, guided by a fence. For safety, a clear Lexan guard fits between the fence and a back support, and a wood exit guard covers the blade where it comes through the fence. A stop can also be added to the side of the saw table or on the outfeed support to keep the box from going so far that the blade cuts through the exit guard.

It's not difficult to make a sliding crosscut box. My first box was a crude carriage made primarily to handle wide work, such as tabletops and chest sides. I made it from a piece of ½-in. plywood and two poplar 2x4s. I was thrilled with how easily the box handled these awkward cutting tasks. At first I used it only for large work. However, most

A sliding crosscut box is a great improvement over the miter gauge in terms of both safety and performance.

Making a sliding crosscut box

A sliding crosscut box must be made of stable material; I made mine from high-quality, nine-ply, ½-in. thick Baltic-birch plywood. Although the midsize box shown in the drawing on p. 126 was made for my Delta Unisaw, the design can be easily adapted to any table saw and to any size workpiece. The accuracy of the crosscut box depends on alignment: The sawblade must be parallel to the miter-gauge slots (see pp. 51-53), and the box's fence must be perpendicular to the blade's line of cut.

Cutting the parts
Cut out the components of the box to the sizes indicated in the drawing, or to fit your own saw. The base should be 1 in. wider than the saw table; the fence and support should be the same length as the base.

Laminate the 1-in. thick fence and back support out of two pieces of plywood. Joint their bottom edges square and cut a ⅛-in. rabbet along the fence's inside bottom edge for sawdust clearance. On the inner face of the fence and back support, cut ¼-in. wide by ¼-in. deep dadoes to receive the ends of the blade guards: a standard guard and an auxiliary guard for cutting tenons and other joints (see p. 162). Then bandsaw the fence and support to the dimensions in the drawing (proportion yours to your saw table). The fence is

higher in the center to hold a workpiece vertically (to cut finger joints and open mortise-and-tenon joints) and lower on the ends so you can clamp narrow pieces to the box.

The runners must be made of a hard, stable material. I used Osage-orange runners on my crosscut box, but any vertical-grain hardwood or plastic will work as well. Rip the runners to fit snugly side to side in the miter-gauge slots, but leave them thinner than the depth of the slots so the base of the box can sit flat on the table. (Most table saws have ¾-in. wide by ⅜-in. deep slots.) After screwing the base to the runners, as described below, you can scrape them until they slide easily.

Attaching the base to the runners
Insert the runners in the miter-gauge slots and place the base on top of them with its front edge aligned with the front edge of the saw table and its left edge extending 1 in. beyond the saw table. Mark the base over the runners' centerline, then drill pilot holes and countersink for #8 by ¾-in. flat-head screws about every 4 in., alternating the screws ¹⁄₁₆ in. on either side of the line to avoid splitting the runner.

Remove the base from the table, then cut off the runners' excess length and scrape the high spots on the edges until the runners slide snugly in the slots. Rub the runners and the underside of the base with wax to seal and lubricate.

Attaching the back support and fence
Fasten the base to the back support with #10 by 2-in. flat-head screws spaced about 3 in. apart, avoiding the dadoes for the Lexan guard and the spot where the blade will cut through the support. The back support doesn't need to be exactly square to the blade. Then slide the fixture into the slots and cut a kerf in the base, stopping a few inches short of the front.

For your crosscut box to be accurate, the fence must be absolutely straight, flat and square to the sawblade. Use a square to check that the face of the fence is perpendicular to the base. Joint the edge if it's not, and recut the rabbet if necessary.

Accurate squaring of the fence to the saw kerf is easy, but it takes some patience. Drill an oversized hole through the base into both ends of the fence. Temporarily fasten the base to either end with one screw from underneath, aligning the fence at 90° to the saw kerf in the base. Before drilling for the rest of the screws, replace the box on the saw and cut through a wide scrap piece. Test the cut with a square; if you need to adjust the fence, loosen the screws in the enlarged holes, tap the fence into alignment, and again cut and check the test piece. Continue this process until you're satisfied that the fence is exactly square, and then drill for and drive the rest of the screws at 3-in. intervals.

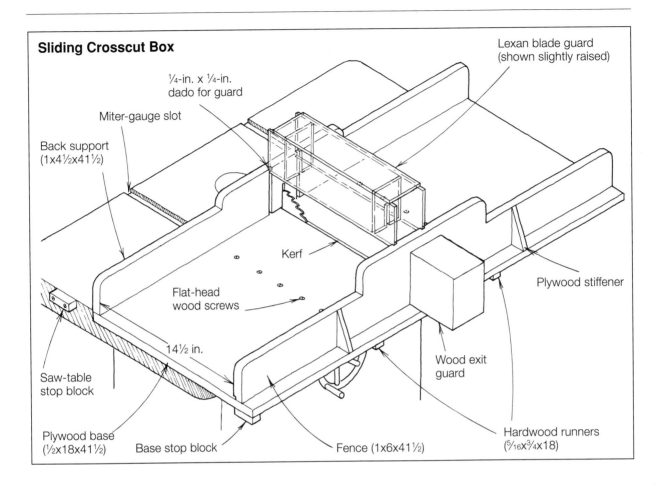

Sliding Crosscut Box

Lexan blade guard (shown slightly raised)

¼-in. x ¼-in. dado for guard

Miter-gauge slot

Back support (1x4½x41½)

Kerf

Flat-head wood screws

Plywood stiffener

14½ in.

Saw-table stop block

Wood exit guard

Plywood base (½x18x41½)

Base stop block

Fence (1x6x41½)

Hardwood runners (⁵⁄₁₆x³⁄₄x18)

Triangular plywood stiffeners help maintain squareness and strengthen the fence. Keep them about 8 in. in from the ends of the fence so you can still clamp an extension board to the fence when repetitively cutting stock to the same length (see p. 132).

Making the blade guard and stop blocks

A blade guard for the crosscut box is a necessity. It shields your fingers and helps protect you from offcuts and sawdust that may fly off the blade. I made my guard out of ¼-in. Lexan, an impact-resistant polycarbonate, but you could also use a clear

acrylic plastic like Plexiglas. Cut the parts to size on the table saw and assemble them with a suitable adhesive. (For the Lexan you can use Weldon 3 solvent cement or Weldon 35, made by IPS, P.O. Box 379, Gardena, Calif. 90248; 213-321-6515.)

Since the blade comes through the fence for all crosscuts, you should make a solid-wood exit guard to protect your fingers. The exit guard should be 2 in. to 3 in. wide, at least ¼ in. above the blade at its maximum height, and at least 1 in. longer than the blade when the blade is centered on the face of the front fence.

Fasten the exit guard to the box with two screws through the fence and two screws through the base. At this point all the wood can be coated with the finish of your choice; I used oil and wax.

Now fasten stop blocks to the box and saw table, as shown in the drawing, so you won't saw through the exit guard. The block on the edge of the saw table should stop the box when the center of the fully raised blade reaches the face of the fence.

crosscutting and joinery done at the table saw involve fairly narrow pieces that are less than 14 in. wide, so I made myself a scaled-down crosscut box, which is much easier to handle. Besides this midsize box (discussed in the sidebar on pp. 125-126), I've also made a box with 12-in. capacity and a large model with 36-in. capacity.

Standard crosscutting

Over the years, the process of crosscutting in my shop has evolved through a number of stages to the point where I use a miter gauge only on rare occasions. Although my preference for the sliding crosscut box should be obvious by now, I'll first describe how to crosscut a board to length with a miter gauge.

Before you begin crosscutting, it's a good idea to move the rip fence to the outer edge of the table (or remove it entirely) so it won't interfere with the cutoff pieces. Never use the rip fence to stop the length of a crosscut—the cutoff piece may wedge between the fence and the blade, resulting in kickback.

Making the cut

Set the blade height, as described on p. 100. Place the guard over the blade and put on your safety gear. With the workpiece against the body of the miter gauge and pulled back away from the blade, turn on the saw and allow the blade to reach full speed.

When only one piece is needed, first cut far enough in from one end of the workpiece to obtain a square end. Don't try to trim the end off square—if the blade is cutting only on the outside it can deflect, leaving the end out of square. When the cut is complete, return the workpiece and miter gauge to the starting point. Slide the wood slightly away from the blade as it is returned to avoid hitting the workpiece against the blade.

Even though you have set the miter gauge square to the blade (see p. 59), it's still a good idea to check the sawn end for square. Sometimes simply altering the pushing action to one side or the other will affect the outcome of the cut. Once you've established a square end, measure the finished length from that end and mark it with a sharp pencil on the edge, using a square as a guide.

Blades for crosscutting

Crosscutting and ripping are fundamentally different operations, and with steel blades require different tooth configurations (see pp. 24-26). With carbide blades, which don't rely on set, tooth configuration is less critical. Blades for crosscutting slice the fibers to either side of the cut and then remove the wood in between. Unless the material is plywood or a veneer, I use a high-quality 40- to 60-tooth ATB blade for crosscutting. A combination blade will also produce acceptable results.

If you are using an auxiliary fence that's even with the blade, you could line up a face mark on the workpiece with the end of the fence and then cut the piece to finished length. Another method is to mark the table in line with the blade, but after a little practice you'll have no trouble sighting the marked line on the workpiece with the blade.

Crosscutting with the sliding crosscut box is essentially the same as crosscutting using a miter gauge. Since the saw's guard cannot be used with the box, I designed my own custom guard, as explained in the sidebar on pp. 125-126. With the runners of the crosscut box positioned in the miter-gauge slots, lift the guard and place the straight edge of your workpiece against the fence so that the end you want to cut is in line with the blade. Push the box forward and cut one end of the wood. Now mark your piece's length and align this mark with the kerf in the carriage of the box, making sure to keep the kerf on the waste side of the cut. Hold the piece against the fence and push the box past the sawblade until the piece is cut.

Stance

When crosscutting a board to length using the miter gauge, stand to the same side of the blade that the gauge is on. (When using the crosscut box, stand to the side that the workpiece is on.) This position is safer and makes for better handling. Use one hand to hold the piece with its straight edge snug against the body of the miter gauge, while the other pushes the gauge in line with its slot (or slots, if using a

When crosscutting, stand behind the miter gauge to the side of the blade.

crosscut box). Don't be tempted to guide the cutoff end of the work with one hand as you are pushing the miter gauge with the other. As the workpiece is cut, stand in the same position as for ripping—to the side of the blade, out of harm's way.

Crosscutting offers less resistance than ripping, so it's tempting to feed the workpiece too fast. In crosscutting, the speed of feed depends on the thickness and hardness of the material being cut, but generally it's not quite as fast as for ripping. A steady, continuous feed that doesn't allow the blade to exit too fast at the end of the cut is best.

Repetitive crosscutting

Making repetitive cuts to the same length is a common practice in woodworking, and there are several ways to set up for these cuts on the table saw. Most setups involve securing some sort of stop block the desired distance from the blade, which eliminates the need to mark the length of individual pieces.

Using a miter gauge, my preferred method for repetitive crosscuts is to clamp an L-shaped stop block to the saw table, as shown in the photo below. The distance between the inside of the L-stop and the blade sets the finished length of the workpiece. For example, if you want to cut a 4-ft. length from a 5-ft. rough board, first clamp the L-stop at 4 ft.

One way to make repetitive cuts to length is to use a long L-stop block. Crosscut one end square, then place the squared end against the L-stop and cut the other end to length.

Without using the L-stop, cut one end of the board square. Then move the miter gauge back, flip the board over and butt the squared-off end against the L-stop. Make a second cut and you have a 4-ft. board with squared ends.

I like the L-stop because it allows me to cut one end square and the other end to length with a single setup. The stop can be made in various lengths and can be used on the saw table for short work or clamped to extend out from the saw for longer pieces. When setting the distance out from the saw use a folding rule that won't sag. Once the stop is clamped you can tap it forward or back to fine-tune the distance to the blade.

Variations on the L-stop include clamping a reference stop at the front of the rip fence and making repetitive cuts. Alternatively, a reference block clamped directly to the saw table keeps cutoff pieces from bunching up in the space between the blade and fence. Both of these methods have one drawback: You have to hold the work firmly so that it doesn't move when it leaves the reference block or during the cut. It's not that difficult a task, but I never hit 100% accuracy when I cut a stack of pieces.

Using a stop block on the auxiliary fence of the miter gauge has the advantage of guiding the workpiece through the cut. The longer the workpiece, the longer the auxiliary fence you need (for more on cross-cutting long stock, see p. 133). You can clamp the block to the fence (as shown in the photo below), but this method requires that one end

Repetitive cuts can be made using a stop block clamped on the auxiliary fence, provided that one end of the workpiece has already been squared.

of the workpiece be already square. A better method is to use a drop stop, which you can flip up to cut one end square and then flip down to cut the workpiece to length.

In my shop, I invariably use the sliding crosscut box equipped with a stop for repetitive crosscutting. The stop block is clamped to the fence the required distance from the blade (either to the left or right of the blade). I keep a block handy that is notched at the bottom for chip clearance. Cut an end of the workpiece square from one side of the box, slide the piece over to the stop and cut it to length. The cutoff

To use the sliding crosscut box for repetitive crosscutting, first square one end of the workpiece from one side of the box (above). Slide the workpiece over to a stop block set the required distance from the blade and make a second cut (right).

piece is carried past the blade along with the workpiece and brought back to the starting position when the cut is complete, where it can be safely removed and dropped in the scrap receptacle at your saw. When I cut a stack of duplicate parts using this setup, I can be confident that they will all be square and cut to exactly the same length.

When you need to cut pieces that are longer than the fence on the crosscut box, clamp an extension board to the fence. Then clamp a stop block to the extension so you can make repetitive cuts. Fence extensions should be made out of a light and stable material, such as poplar or mahogany. They should be thick enough not to flex and tall enough to clamp to the box above the stock.

I have recently installed parts of the FastTrack stop system (available from Garrett Wade) to one of my cutoff boxes for easy and accurate repetitive crosscuts (see the photos below). I adapted the aluminum extruded track to the fence of the box, and ran a shallow groove in the face of the fence so I could add a rule to either side of the blade. Now I have dual drop stops with a micro-adjuster always at hand that I can move anywhere along the fence.

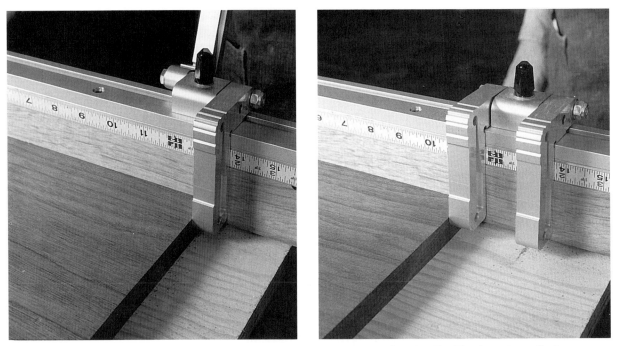

To make repetitive crosscuts using the FastTrack system, first square one end with the board against the outside stop (left). Then flip the inside stop down and cut the board to length (right).

Crosscutting wide panels

Crosscutting wide panels using only a miter gauge for support is inaccurate and awkward, so I always use a crosscut box for this operation. The crosscut box really shines here, since it carries the work across the table instead of your having to push the weight of it. If you have been cutting wide and heavy work with only a miter gauge, you'll really appreciate the crosscut box's ease of handling as well as the results.

The procedure is essentially the same as for standard crosscutting, but with a larger crosscut box. With the guard in place, square off one end, then cut the panel to length, lining up the mark on the workpiece with the kerf in the crosscut box. On very wide work, I sometimes start the cut by raising the blade up through the wood. This way of working is easier and safer than pulling the crosscut box out over the front of the saw in order to start in front of a raised blade.

If the work is not only wide but also long (such as a tabletop or case side), you'll need some form of support to keep the workpiece flat on the carriage while it is being cut. One way to accomplish this is to use an outfeed support table to the side of the saw. My preferred method is to clamp a thick block of wood to the fence to keep the panel from lifting off the carriage.

Wide panels can be crosscut on the table saw using a large version of the crosscut box. A wood block clamped to the fence holds the board down against the base of the box.

One other consideration when cutting wide work is supporting the crosscut box as it goes over the back of the saw. For a number of years I made do with my adjustable overarm-router table situated as a support. I finally attached a large outfeed table to my saw with grooves that line up with the miter slots in the table (see p. 42). This wonderful addition supports the crosscut box and all work coming off the saw. I have also used commercial outfeed rollers and fold-down tables that attach to the back of the saw.

Crosscutting short pieces

Crosscutting short pieces on the table saw can be a dangerous operation because your fingers are that much closer to the blade than with longer work. The safest way to cut short pieces is with the crosscut box. Use a wooden hold-down to secure the workpiece against the fence and make the cut with the clear guard in place (as shown in the photo below). You could also cut short pieces with a hold-down and an auxiliary fence on the miter gauge, but the guard cannot be used for this operation and the small cutoff is more difficult to deal with than on the crosscut box. One other option, of course, is to cut short pieces of wood at your workbench with a handsaw.

Crosscut very short workpieces using a crosscut box and a wooden hold-down.

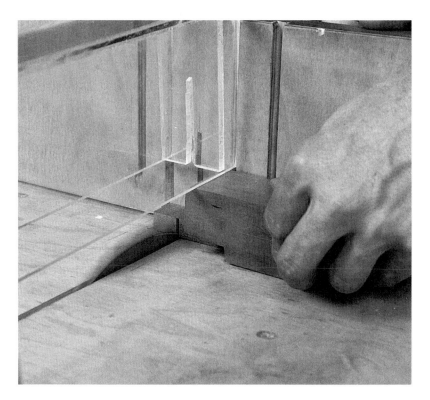

Crosscutting bevels

Bevel crosscuts, sometimes called end miters, are produced by crosscutting a board with the sawblade tilted at an angle other than 90°. This is a joinery cut that I usually use only for joining molding. Although bevel crosscuts can be used as a corner joint where the design calls for a clean edge, the end miter joins end grain to end grain, and needs reinforcement.

To make bevel crosscuts, tilt the blade to the angle needed (usually 45°) and check the setting with a sliding bevel or drafting triangle. For best results, the cut should be made so that the cutoff ends up below the blade.

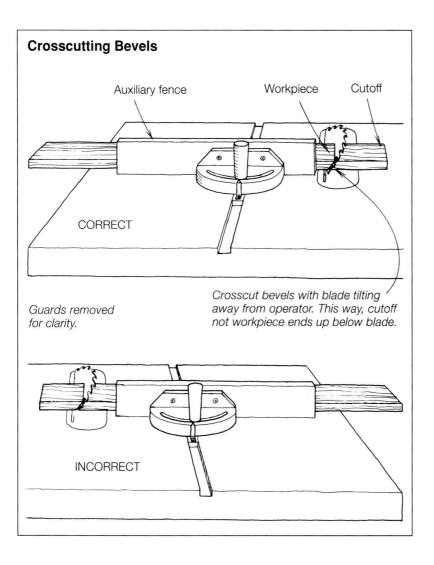

Crosscutting Bevels

Auxiliary fence   Workpiece   Cutoff

CORRECT

Guards removed for clarity.

Crosscut bevels with blade tilting away from operator. This way, cutoff not workpiece ends up below blade.

INCORRECT

The miter gauge can be used to crosscut bevels, but for the sake of accuracy I use a small cutoff box with a blade opening large enough to accommodate a tilted blade. (I don't use this box for straight crosscutting, because small cutoffs could drop into the opening, unless I put a thin piece of plywood on top of the carriage before cutting.)

Crosscutting miters

Miters are produced by feeding the work into the blade at an angle other than 90°. When the sawblade is set at 90° to the table, the cut is a face miter or flat miter. When the sawblade is set at an angle other than 90°, the cut is a compound miter. Miter cuts are used primarily as joints and are discussed in detail on pp. 171-173.

Setting the miter gauge

There are a number of ways to set the miter gauge for miter cuts. One is to use a sliding bevel or a drafting triangle to set the required angle between the body and the bar. Another method is to scribe the angle on the workpiece, then turn over the gauge and set to the scribe mark. A third method is to use the stops or gauge on the miter head. Whichever method you use, test your setup on a piece of scrap wood first.

If you frequently miter at a particular angle, you can make a template by gluing two pieces of wood together at the angle you need. When the glue is dry, screw the pieces together, and save this template to set up the miter gauge next time.

The miter gauge can be set in either the open or closed position (see the drawing on the facing page). I was taught to miter closed, because this position keeps you more out of line with the blade and the cut is smoother because of the orientation of the grain. However, I find that the work is more likely to creep in this position, and your hands get closer to the blade as the angle gets steeper. Adding an auxiliary fence and stop using the open position will yield better results. Cement sandpaper to the fence to keep the workpiece from slipping.

Most miter cutting is done on a number of pieces that fit together, and at least two pairs need to be exactly the same length. Unless the parts you want to miter have already been cut to length or have a square end, you will need two stops to make the procedure work. (Alternatively, you could cut each end without a stop first and then add a stop for the finished dimensions.)

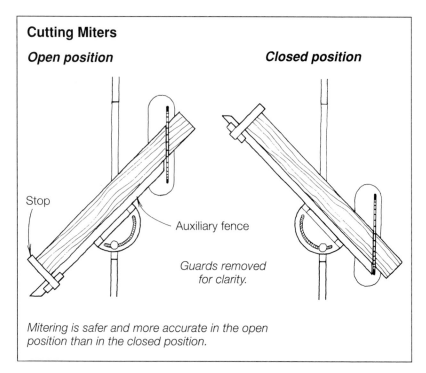

Cutting Miters

Open position   **Closed position**

Stop

Auxiliary fence

*Guards removed
for clarity.*

*Mitering is safer and more accurate in the open
position than in the closed position.*

**Use an auxiliary fence and stop block when cutting miters with a
miter gauge.**

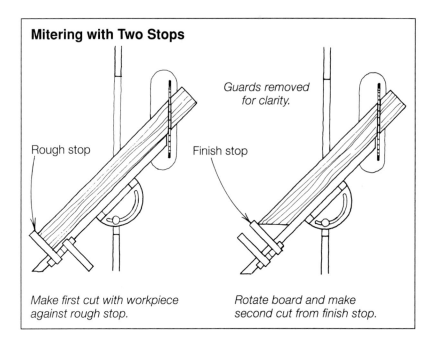

Mitering with Two Stops

Rough stop

Finish stop

Guards removed for clarity.

Make first cut with workpiece against rough stop.

Rotate board and make second cut from finish stop.

The cuts are made by cutting one end from the rough stop and then flipping end for end and cutting from the finish-length stop, as shown in the drawing above. Make sure the stop is wide enough to contact the full width of the workpiece. Since most frames are rectangular you may need to make two setups — one for the long sides and one for the short sides.

Woodworkers use a couple of tricks when cutting miters. Some add a small shim at each stop for the rough cut and remove it for a light smoothing cut. Many woodworkers also cut the last corner joint at whatever angle it takes to get a good fit, since a minor difference in length is a lot less noticeable than a bad joint.

Crosscut box for miters

I find that the miter gauge is inaccurate for cutting miters, which leave so little room for error. Instead, I use a simple shopmade 45° crosscut box. For those rare occasions when I cut a miter at an angle other than 45°, I either fiddle with the miter gauge until I get the cut right or add a spacer or hold-down to my cutoff box to make the cuts.

The best way to cut miters is to use a crosscut box with two fences angled at 45° to the blade. A cutout in the back of the box allows you to miter stock up to 12 in. wide.

The 45° crosscut box is basically the same as the 90° crosscut box, except that the two fences are at 45° to the blade and perpendicular to each other. This jig allows cutting from both sides; if the two angles add up to 90°, the miter joint will fit well, even if neither angle is 45°. You can extend the fences to accommodate length stops where needed.

Face miters such as those used in a picture frame are cut at a 45° angle. Four pieces cut at this angle will make a square or a rectangle. When joining more than four sides to make a frame, you can calculate the cutting angle by dividing 180° by the number of sides. For example, a six-sided piece has 30° angles.

If you cut a lot of miters, it's worth making a box to handle the required angle. If you have a lot of different angles to cut, I would strongly recommend adding a small sliding cutoff saw to your workshop. Sliding cutoff saws are specifically designed for cutting miters and now are reasonably priced.

CHAPTER 8
Table-Saw Joinery

Crisp, accurate joinery is the hallmark of fine furniture, and the table saw can help you achieve it. The table saw can be used for cutting many joints, more than I could possibly write about in one chapter. I have narrowed them down to the ones I am most familiar with and the ones that use the table saw as the main cutting tool.

A word of warning before we begin: Old woodworking books and magazines suggest a lot of different operations in addition to joinery that are possible to do on the table saw, but that doesn't necessarily mean that the table saw is the best machine for the job. Avoid operations like gouging out bowls, cutting circles, resawing wide stock, making dowels and shaping on the table saw, which are inefficient at best and downright dangerous at worst. There are usually better ways to do the same operations without taking unnecessary risks.

Strength is a primary goal of joinery, and strength in a glue joint comes from long-grain to long-grain contact in the pieces being joined. To get this contact it is important that the surfaces be very smooth. Rough surfaces are held apart by the loose fibers and small air pockets and

Shopmade jigs and fixtures make it possible to cut a wide variety of joints on the table saw. Shown here is a simple jig for cutting finger joints.

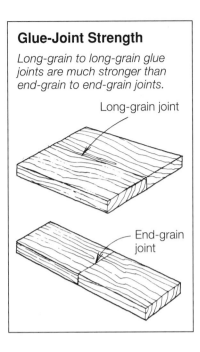
consequently make for a weaker joint. The reason that end-grain surfaces make for weak joints is that end grain is mostly open holes. These tend to draw the glue away from the surfaces, and the small amount of wood fibers at the ends of the cell walls is not sufficient to make a strong bond.

Of course, there is more to joinery than gluing. To counteract the many different stresses that a joint may have to withstand, mechanical components are also needed. Shoulders, mortises and tenons, and locking techniques such as dovetails combine with surface bonding to make a complete joint.

The condition and type of cutting tool play a big part in good joinery. The plane, chisel, jointer and router generally make for a smoother gluing surface than the handsaw, table saw and bandsaw. However, a well-tuned table saw equipped with the appropriate sharp blade can produce a very satisfactory gluing surface. For most of my table-saw joinery, I use a sharp 40-tooth carbide ATB blade (see p. 25). If I experience tearout when making test cuts across the grain, I switch to a finer 60-tooth ATB crosscut blade.

Edge joints

Edge-to-edge joints, the simplest of woodworking joints, are used primarily to make wider panels from narrower boards, as in tabletops and case sides. Edge joints can be reinforced with splines, dowels or biscuits, but most modern wood glues are all that is necessary for a strong joint, provided the joint is well made.

Butt joint

Making a butt, or plain edge, joint is a simple ripping operation that can be followed by smoothing the edge on the jointer. To get a good joint at the saw, use a steel rip blade with very little set (see p. 20) or a carbide-tipped blade with minimum side clearance. Make sure your rip fence is set parallel to the blade, or use a half-fence (see pp. 95-97) so that both pieces to be joined end up as smooth as possible.

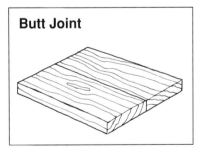
A good edge joint must be straight and square to the face of both boards along their full length. I test the fit of the joint by placing both edge surfaces together to see if they swivel. If they move easily, the center of the joint is high and contact is not being made at the ends. In a good joint there will be drag as you swivel the top board.

Ideally, I like a butt joint that is just a bit hollow toward the center—this is known as a "spring joint." Even with well-dried wood and a good glue joint the ends of boards take on and give up moisture more readily than the rest of the panel. A clamped spring joint puts more pressure at the ends, where the joint is most likely to fail as the wood expands and contracts. You can make this joint by ripping a board at the table saw and then smoothing and relieving the center with a shallow pass from a plane. Alternatively, you can cut the spring joint by using a jointer that has been adjusted so that the outfeed table is slightly higher than the jointer knives. The maximum gap recommended is a combined $\frac{1}{32}$ in. for 4-ft. boards (and less for shorter boards).

Just in case the sawblade is not at a perfect 90° to the saw table, it's a good habit to alternate the marked face side of your boards to the table so that any deviation will make a complementary joint. (It's not necessary to do this, however, if you are running the boards through the jointer after the table-saw cut.)

Splined edge joint

Splined edge joints come in handy for aligning long boards and random-width back panels. They are made by cutting matching grooves in the pieces to be joined, then cutting the spline (a long, thin piece) and gluing it into the grooves when the panel is assembled (random-width backs don't get glued). I usually cut the splined edge joint by using a single sawblade to form a groove on the adjoining edges. (A dado head can be used for wider grooves.) The stock could be turned to the opposite face to center a wider groove, but pieces do not always come prepared to the exact same thickness, so the size of the groove would vary. It's a better practice to work from the marked face for all cutting and either move the fence or add a spacer stick for any additional cutting. Material thicker than $1\frac{1}{4}$ in. calls for two grooves.

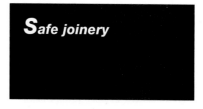

Safe joinery

An inherent problem when cutting joinery at the table saw is the lack of safety equipment for many of the procedures. Many of the cuts are difficult or impossible to make with the standard guard assembly in place.

I find it especially important to use a guard while making joinery cuts. Whenever you have to work around an exposed blade, there is danger. In table-saw joinery you have to handle workpieces on end, on edge and at odd angles; you may have to make deep cuts with the blade more exposed than usual (a sure sign of danger). However, in the spirit of safe sawing, it's not too difficult to devise guards for most joinery procedures, as you'll see from the examples in this chapter. I'm sure that the ingenious woodworker will be able to come up with good if not better solutions as well.

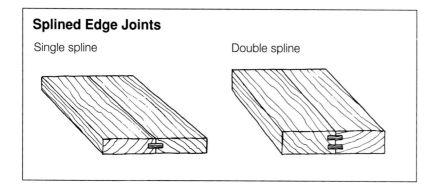

Splined Edge Joints

Single spline   Double spline

The groove for the splined edge joint can be cut safely with a
featherboard holding the workpiece against the rip fence.

In order to cut the grooves, you have to stand the workpiece on edge.
Use a featherboard to help hold the board steady (and a high auxiliary
fence if the workpiece is tall). Normally a featherboard is placed just in
front of the blade to keep the saw kerf from closing onto the blade, but
for this cut I find it better to place the featherboard directly opposite
the blade, where it acts as a partial blade guard, since this cut cannot
be made with the standard guard.

One blade guard that can be used when making grooving cuts is the
Brett-Guard (see pp. 77-78). You can butt this guard right up against
the workpiece and it will cover the blade when it is exposed at the beginning and end of the cut. If you are grooving a long workpiece,
which is likely to have some warp, you are better off with a long board
clamped across the saw table to act as a guide and keep the work flat
during the cut.

Marking the workpiece

If you are cutting joints on your table saw, you will need a system for marking the workpiece so you can easily determine the sides you want showing in the finished project, the square faces and edges you will use as references for layout, the locations of the joints, and the areas that will be removed. You'll be less likely to make mistakes if you use a simple marking method.

Woodworkers use various systems, from squiggly lines (to indicate square edges) to triangles to Xs and Os; some also number sequenced parts. It's not unusual to write the name of the parts on the pieces, especially in the rough-milling stage, when the parts are not easily identifiable. I also mark the face side of the workpiece for grain direction (both before and after the wood is glued up) to minimize tearouts during planing and jointing.

Marking the Workpiece

Squiggly lines indicate square edges.

Simple marks or triangles can be used as glue-up reference and to show position of face sides.

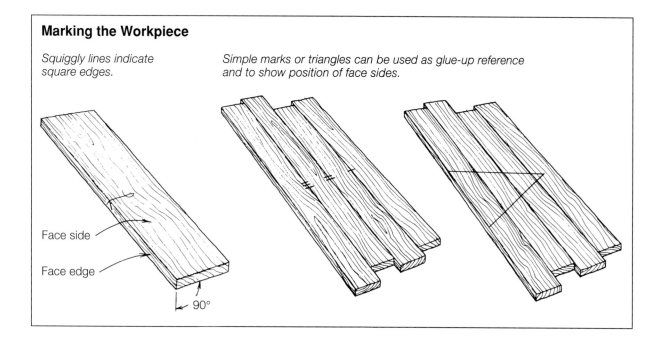

Face side

Face edge

90°

To cut the groove, first mark the center of the workpiece, align the mark with the center of the blade or dado cutter and set the rip fence. (It's not critical that the groove end up right in the center, but it is important that the grooves line up exactly with each other.)

Adjust the height of the blade to allow for half the width of the spline plus about $1/32$ in. for glue space. The spline's width is usually equal to the thickness of the material being joined, but not usually more than $3/4$ in. The spline can be made up of shorter lengths if necessary.

Splines are cut from plywood or solid wood ripped from the edges of ¾-in. wood, using the jig for narrow ripping (see pp. 110-111). Plywood makes stronger splines than long-grain solid wood. I do use matching solid wood when making spline-and-groove cabinet backs, however, since the splines are visible when the boards shrink.

The fit of the spline in the groove is important. If the spline is too wide, the joint won't pull together; if it is too narrow, the joint loses strength; and if the spline is too thick, the joint will spread. The fit is right when the spline can be pushed in lightly by hand. Easing the spline's edges a little with a sanding block eliminates any splinters that might hold up the spline at glue-up.

Hidden spline joint

A hidden spline is the same as a splined edge, except that the spline and groove don't show in the assembled joint. It's a useful joint when you don't want to see the groove at the end of the boards, as in a tabletop. You can make a stopped groove on the table saw. The procedure is the same as for a through groove, except that you start cutting beyond one end and stop before you reach the other end. This sort of "drop-in" work is done frequently on the table saw and is safe as long as the cut is shallow and narrow (it's not something you should try with a deep dado or molding head). Stop blocks clamped to the fence register the start and stop points and also help resist any tendency for kickback, especially on small workpieces.

Lay out the groove by marking the starting and stopping points of the cut on the workpiece. Because the layout line will be against the table surface as you make the cut, use a square to transfer the layout marks to the outside of one of the boards. These marks will help you install the stop blocks on the rip fence.

Now raise the sawblade or dado head to the desired height, and move the rip fence against it. Use a pencil and a square to mark lightly on the fence the points at which the teeth at the front and back of the blade pass through the throat plate. These marks indicate the beginning and end of the cutting arc. (A fence faced with plastic laminate is useful here, since the pencil marks erase easily.)

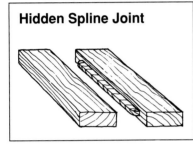

Hidden Spline Joint

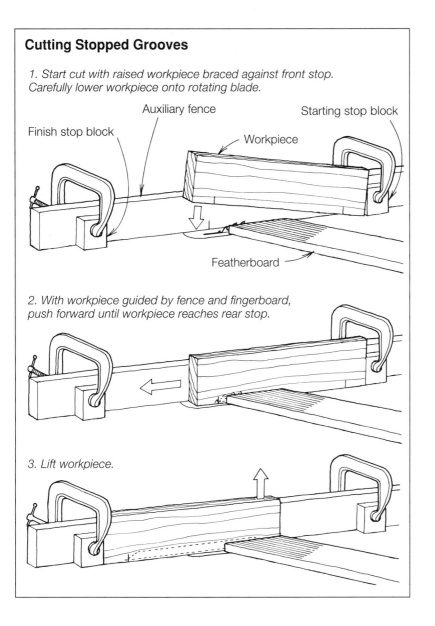

Cutting Stopped Grooves

1. Start cut with raised workpiece braced against front stop. Carefully lower workpiece onto rotating blade.

Auxiliary fence

Finish stop block

Starting stop block

Workpiece

Featherboard

2. With workpiece guided by fence and fingerboard, push forward until workpiece reaches rear stop.

3. Lift workpiece.

Next, move the rip fence the desired distance from the cutter, and lower the blade. Place the workpiece on the table so that its front mark is aligned with the mark on the rip fence at the back of the blade, and clamp a stop block on the fence at the back edge of the stock. This is the starting block. Now move the stock so that the back mark on the workpiece aligns with the mark on the rip fence at the front of the blade, and clamp the second stop block at the front edge, as shown in the drawing above.

With the stop blocks in place and the fence and sawblade set, you are ready to make the cut. Turn the saw on, and guide the workpiece straight down along the auxiliary fence and against the starting block. Using a featherboard as described on p. 144 will help guide the workpiece onto the blade. Continue with the cut until the work reaches the finish stop block, then carefully lift it off, picking the back end up first.

If your workpiece is longer than the capacity of the rip fence, as in some tabletops, you won't be able to use stop blocks. This is not a problem, because you can work to marks on the table-saw surface. The wood will be heavy enough to counteract the force of cutting the narrow groove and won't kick back as might a small board dropped onto the blade. If you prefer, you can also add an extended auxiliary fence (see p. 107).

Once the groove is cut, you can either round the ends of the spline to fit the groove or square off the ends of the groove with a chisel. An alternative to the hidden spline is to cut the groove through and glue in decorative or matching wood. Saved cutoffs can make an inlay that will be almost invisible.

Rabbets, dadoes and grooves

Three types of cuts — the rabbet, the dado and the groove — are frequently used in constructing furniture and cabinets, and all of them can be cut on the table saw. A rabbet is a rectangular cut made on an edge or end of a board. A dado is a rectangular slot, cut on the face of a board, that runs across the grain. A groove is similar to a dado except that it runs with the grain either on the face or edge of a board. Nowadays, woodworkers often make these cuts with the router, but there are still some advantages to using the table saw — you can make deeper cuts in a single pass with the table saw, and it's better than the router for cutting exact widths.

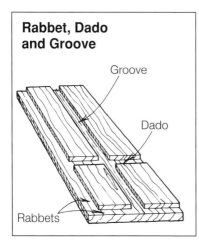

Rabbet, Dado and Groove

Groove

Dado

Rabbets

Rabbet

A rabbet can be used at the back of case sides to attach either a frame-and-panel, plywood or tongue-and-groove back. You can also cut a rabbet to leave a tongue that can be one part of a tongue-and-dado joint, as in the back of a drawer or a shelf (see pp. 152-153). And rabbeted edges can fit together to form a dustproof door joint. There are two ways to cut rabbets on the table saw — in two passes using a single sawblade, or in one pass with a dado blade.

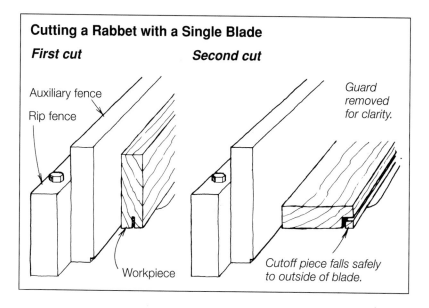

Cutting a Rabbet with a Single Blade

First cut

Second cut

Auxiliary fence

Rip fence

Guard removed for clarity.

Workpiece

Cutoff piece falls safely to outside of blade.

Rabbet with a single sawblade The two-pass method of cutting a rabbet with a single blade works best if the pieces to be joined are the same width, because the fence has to be reset for the second cut for every piece that is a different width. Make the first cut with the workpiece on edge and the second cut with the board flat on the table. This second cut must be made with the workpiece positioned so that the cutoff piece ends up on the outside of the blade, as shown in the drawing above. If the cutoff piece falls between the blade and the fence, it can bind and kick back.

Another method for cutting a rabbet with a single sawblade involves using an auxiliary fence raised slightly above the saw table, as shown in the photos on p. 150. Raising the auxiliary fence prevents cutoff pieces from being trapped and kicked back by the sawblade. This is the method I prefer when rabbeting a number of pieces of different widths, because you don't need to reset the rip fence for the second cut more than once (and not at all if you're cutting a square rabbet).

For the first cut, set the blade height to the width of the rabbet, and set the distance from the fence to the outside of the blade to the depth of the rabbet. For the second cut, place the workpiece face down on the table and set the distance from the fence to the outside of the blade equal to the depth of the rabbet.

Rabbets can be cut in two passes, using an auxiliary fence raised slightly above the saw table so the cutoff piece doesn't get wedged between the blade and the fence.

Rabbeting with a dado head requires only one pass over the blade.

As when cutting the groove for the splined edge joint (see p. 144), you can support the work for the first cut using a featherboard, the Brett-Guard or a long board clamped across the table. For the second cut, I like to clamp a wood guard fence to the rip fence to hold the work flat, as shown in the bottom photo on the facing page.

To cut a rabbet on the end of a board, make the first cut as just described. For the second cut, which in this case is a crosscut, use a miter gauge equipped with an auxiliary fence (or a sliding crosscut box) to guide the work.

Rabbet with a dado blade   If you have a number of pieces to rabbet, it's a lot easier to cut the joint in a single pass with a dado head. The cut is made with the workpiece held flat on the table by a wooden hold-down/guard, as shown in the photo above. You will need a wooden auxiliary fence attached to the rip fence and the appropriate throat plate to accommodate the wider dado blade.

To make the cut, first set the dado head a little wider than the width of the rabbet that you want. Lower the blade and move the fence so that the distance between the fence and the far side of the blade equals the width of the rabbet. A small part of the dado head will be buried in the wood auxiliary fence as you raise the blade to a height equal to the depth of the rabbet. Feed the workpiece over the blade to cut the rabbet.

For a rabbet wider than the capacity of the dado head, move the fence over for a second cut. To cut an end rabbet with a dado head, use the miter gauge or a sliding crosscut box. If you find that the workpiece is tearing out across the grain (sheet material tends to be a problem), make a light scoring cut first, with the blade just barely above the table.

Tongue and dado

The bare-faced tongue and dado (or tongue and groove) is used where a tongue would weaken the edge of the side that it is cut into, as in a case top, case back or drawer back. It is a lightweight joint that can work well on small projects and plywood fixtures. The joint is stronger if the dado is set in slightly so that the mating pieces are not flush at the outside corner (see the drawing at left).

As a rule, the depth of the dado and the thickness of the tongue are equal to one-quarter the thickness of their respective parts (for example, $3/4$-in. thick pieces would have a $3/16$-in. tongue and a $3/16$-in. deep dado). The joint can be cut with either a dado head or a single blade. I usually use a single blade, as described below, for cuts that are $1/4$ in. deep or less.

To cut a bare-faced tongue and dado (or tongue and groove) that is flush with the end or edge, first set the fence so that the distance to the outside of the blade equals the thickness of the piece with the tongue (see the top drawing on the facing page). Set the blade height equal to the depth of the dado. If the joint isn't flush, set the blade height and move the fence so that the blade will cut the groove where needed. To cut the dado, hold the end of the workpiece snugly against the fence and use the miter gauge to guide the board over the blade. To cut a groove, simply use the fence as a guide.

Bare-Faced Tongue and Dado

Good   Better

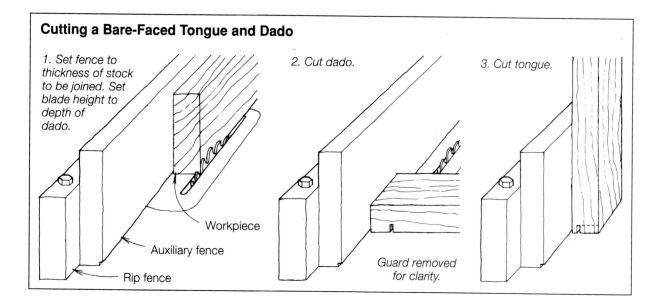

Cutting a Bare-Faced Tongue and Dado

1. Set fence to thickness of stock to be joined. Set blade height to depth of dado.

2. Cut dado.

3. Cut tongue.

Workpiece

Auxiliary fence

Rip fence

Guard removed for clarity.

Cut the matching tongue just as you would cut a rabbet, using either two passes with a single blade or one pass with a dado head (see pp. 149-152). You have to reset the fence, but the blade can be left at the same height to produce a tongue the same length as the dado depth (or you can drop the blade height a hair to allow for gluing).

I sometimes use the bare-faced tongue-and-groove joint to fit the bottoms of drawers, especially if they are solid wood. This joint, which is not glued, allows for a thicker drawer bottom without the need to cut a wide groove in the bottom of the drawer sides and front. I make the bottoms $\frac{3}{8}$ in. to $\frac{1}{2}$ in. thick and use a $\frac{1}{4}$-in. thick tongue. To make the $\frac{1}{4}$-in. groove in the sides and front with a single $\frac{1}{8}$-in. kerf blade, I clamp a $\frac{1}{8}$-in. spacer stick to the rip fence and cut the first groove. Then I remove the spacer and cut again, to produce a $\frac{1}{4}$-in. groove for the drawer bottom. Finally, I raise the blade and cut through the back piece so that the drawer bottom will just pass under the back when it is slid into the grooves in the sides and front.

Housed dado

Dadoes are frequently used to house the full end of a shelf—anything from a small, thin shelf in a desk compartment to a full-sized shelf in a bookcase. I also use this joint to house drawer supports in the sides of chest cases. The housed dado is not a particularly strong joint, but as long as the case is held firmly together, it can support a lot of weight.

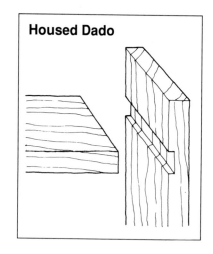

Housed Dado

One way to cut a through dado is to guide the workpiece across the
dado head with a sliding crosscut box.

To cut the housed dado joint, set the width of the dado blade equal to the thickness of the shelf or frame member that is to fit into the dado. Set the blade height equal to the required depth of cut, which should be about one-third the thickness of the piece. You can use a miter gauge fitted with an auxiliary fence to cut the dado, but I prefer to use a crosscut box with a wide saw kerf designed specifically for dado cutting (as shown in the photos on the facing page).

Check the accuracy of the setup by cutting a dado on a scrap piece of stock. You may need to add paper washers between the inside chippers to make the cut wider (see pp. 26-27). If so, place the washers evenly between the chippers — bunching them can leave a ridge of wood at the bottom of the dado.

Cutting with a dado head removes a lot more wood than cutting with a single blade, and the potential for kickback is accordingly greater. Feed the stock slowly over the cutters, applying downward pressure so that the work does not climb or lift off the blade. Never place your hands on the workpiece directly over the blade.

Blind dado

The blind dado is used where an exposed dado joint would be unattractive or where a cabinet door is set in a case. Fortunately, for safety's sake, blind dadoing is usually only half blind. Dropping in work on a wide dado set is one of the more dangerous kickback situations and should be avoided at all costs.

In the blind-dado joint, a dado is cut partway across one board; then a corner is notched out of the second board to cover the front of the joint. The curved part at the end of the dado is usually squared off with a hand chisel.

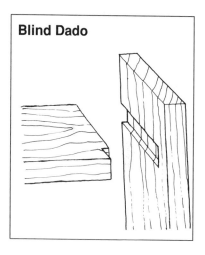

Blind Dado

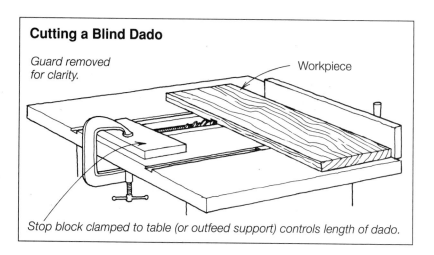

Cutting a Blind Dado

Guard removed for clarity.

Workpiece

Stop block clamped to table (or outfeed support) controls length of dado.

To cut a blind dado, first measure the length of the dado that you want, and then raise the blade to the correct height for the depth of the dado. Mark the point where the blade goes into the saw table at the front of the blade, and measure from this mark a distance equal to the length of the dado. Place a stop in line with the blade at this point, as shown in the bottom drawing on p. 155. (Note that if you use a sliding crosscut box to cut this joint, you'll need a stop to stop the box, not the workpiece.) A strong magnet (from a speaker) works well as a stop, or you can clamp a block to the saw table or outfeed support. Advance the workpiece into the blade and lift it from the table when the front edge contacts the stop.

Edge tongue and groove

Cutting a rabbet on both sides of the edge of a board will leave a tongue, which can fit into a groove in the mating board. The edge tongue and groove is a good joint to use in solid-wood cabinet backs. It is not glued, so the large surface area can move freely. The tongue keeps the case sealed, and a chamfer or roundover along the edges can make the spaces between boards into a decorative feature.

To lay out the tongue, allow one-third of the thickness of the board for the tenon and one-third for each shoulder. The depth of the groove should be about one-half the thickness of the board. Cut the groove as explained on pp. 144-145. Cut the tongue using the same technique as for making a rabbet, using a single blade or dado head (see pp. 149-152). If the back panels are thin enough to make the tongue and shoulders with one operation, I sometimes cut the tongues with two blades held apart by a spacer of wood, Lucite or metal, which will ensure that all the tongues will end up the same thickness even if the thickness of the wood varies.

Full tongue and dado

A full tongue and dado is similar to the edge tongue and groove except that the tongue is made on the end of a board and the dado is made on the face of the mating board. This joint is used primarily in shelf construction. Since the tongue has shoulders, the joint is hidden and the workpiece can be sanded before glue-up without affecting the fit. The shoulders also add strength.

The full tongue and dado is usually made with a blind dado, as described above. The tongue is cut as explained in the edge tongue and groove section.

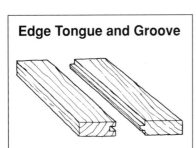

Edge Tongue and Groove

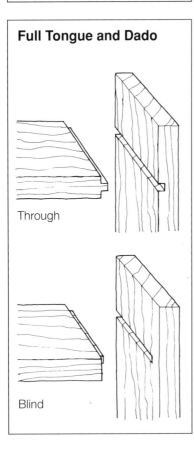

Full Tongue and Dado

Through

Blind

A V-block jig holds the workpiece for cutting a corner dado.

Corner dado

A corner dado is used to house a shelf in the legs of a table. A rectangular groove is cut across the edge of the table leg, and a corner is cut off the shelf to fit in the groove. This joint is not very strong by itself, so a dowel should be run through the leg into the shelf to reinforce it.

To cut the dado in the leg, hold the stock in a V-block jig attached to the miter gauge (as shown in the photo above). The jig has a clear guard on its leading edge. Set the dado head to the desired height and then guide the jig and workpiece over the blade.

Corner Dado

Cutting a Dovetail Dado

1. Cut dado to width of dovetail neck.

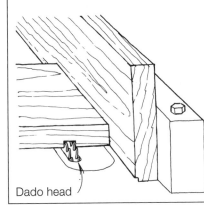

Dado head

2. Make angle cut on either side of dado to form dovetail dado.

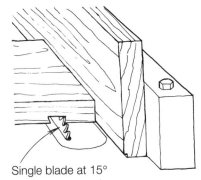

Single blade at 15°

3. Cut shoulders of dovetail tenon.

4. With blade set at 15°, cut cheeks of dovetail tenon.

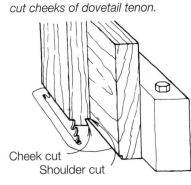

Cheek cut
Shoulder cut

Dovetail Dadoes

Full dovetail dado

Half dovetail dado

Full dovetail dado

The full dovetail dado is similar to a housed dado, but it provides additional mechanical strength in shelf, frame and drawer construction. Although this joint is usually made with a router, it can also be cut on a table saw. To cut the dado, first make a dado to the narrowest width of the dovetail, as shown in the drawing above. Replace the dado head with a single blade and tilt it to an angle of 15°. Make the angle cut on either side to clean out the dado.

To cut the dovetail tenon, first cut the two shoulders. I use the sliding crosscut box for this operation. Set a stop in the crosscut box equal to the depth of the dado. After marking a test piece from the dado, adjust the fence to the mark. Cut the first shoulder, then turn the piece to the opposite face for the second cut. To make the angled cuts, set the blade at 15° and stand the workpiece on end. Use a tenoning jig (see p. 162) to support long workpieces.

I usually make the dovetail slightly oversize to compensate for different thicknesses of wood and then fit each one individually. The half dovetail dado is cut the same way as the full dovetail except that the angled cuts are made on only one side of the joint.

Lap Joints

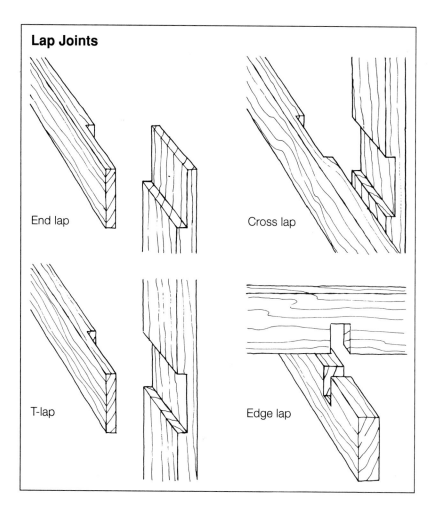

End lap

Cross lap

T-lap

Edge lap

Early in my woodworking education, I was required to cut an end-lap joint from a single piece of oversized poplar using only hand tools. Before we were allowed to move on to any other woodworking, this joint had to fit perfectly together and be square in all planes. This feat took the class almost an entire college quarter; it was not only an exercise in learning to use hand tools but also an example of the patience and care necessary for successful woodworking. (Many overeager students dropped out this first quarter when they discovered that they were not going to be able to start out making furniture.) Since then, I've found little use for the end-lap joint, except for some showroom display stands. But there are other forms of this joint that I have found handy in my cabinetmaking work, especially the edge lap and the dovetail lap.

Lap joints

Lap joints are simple joints that lend themselves to lightweight frame construction. The lap consists of two rabbets, two dadoes or a combination of the two. When the two boards are matched, the thickness at the joint is equal to the full thickness of each board alone. Variations include the end lap, the T-lap, the cross lap, the edge lap, the dovetail lap, the bridle joint and the open mortise and tenon.

End lap

The end lap consists of a matching rabbet at the end of two boards, which are joined at right angles. It is a weak frame joint that is rarely used in quality work because it requires screws for reinforcement (though it is good for shop fixtures, display stands, and so forth). With two opposing grain directions the glue line is apt to fail, especially if the work is wide.

Test pieces come in handy for a number of tasks in the woodshop. Many setups for joinery require test cuts — you want to be sure the setup is accurate before you ruin good wood. The best source for test pieces is cutoffs from the stock you are working on. Cutoffs are also invaluable for making matching repairs or cutting out plugs for covering screw holes. (Sometimes I mark where they were cut from; for example, "right side of top or chest side.") Keep these pieces handy since it can be a couple of days before you get to the operations.

Lap joints can be cut exclusively on the table saw, using either a single blade or a dado set, but I prefer to team up the table saw and the router for a good, clean joint. Even the highest-quality dado head or a single blade will produce rough cheeks that must be pared with a chisel or routed to get two smooth surfaces that will make a good glue bond.

Generally the pieces to be joined are equal in thickness and width. Therefore the width of the cut will equal the width of the piece and the depth of the cut will equal half the thickness. When setting up for the end lap it is wise to lay out the joint first on cutoffs that have the same dimensions as the workpieces. Use a marking gauge to determine the middle of the stock's thickness and mark a test piece. Bring the piece up to the blade and raise the blade or dado set so that a tooth's tip at its apex is to the halfway mark. This setting should leave the cheeks a bit full to allow for cleanup of the roughness. A couple of trial runs on the two test pieces will give you feedback. When the halves are equal, lay out the actual joint by marking one workpiece on the face and the other on the back.

To set the width of cut, I use a stop clamped the correct distance from the blade on an auxiliary fence on the miter gauge or on the crosscut box. You can set the stop by moving the auxiliary fence up to the blade and measuring or placing a piece the same width at the edge of the blade. Cut the shoulder, then remove the rest of the cut making as many overlapping passes as necessary. Clean up the cheeks using a straight bit in the router table.

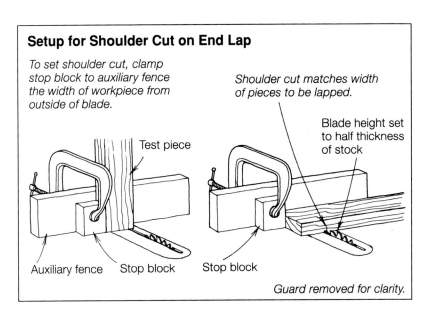

Setup for Shoulder Cut on End Lap

To set shoulder cut, clamp stop block to auxiliary fence the width of workpiece from outside of blade.

Test piece

Shoulder cut matches width of pieces to be lapped.

Blade height set to half thickness of stock

Auxiliary fence   Stop block   Stop block

Guard removed for clarity.

T-laps, cross laps and edge laps are cut in much the same way as end laps. The only difference is in the setup for the position of the lap. For laps that occur in the middle of a board, use two stops to establish the two sides of the lap (as shown in the photos below).

Cut the cross-lap joint on the sliding crosscut box, using stop blocks set to the width of the lap. Make the first cut with both stops flipped down. Then flip the inner stop up and make successive cuts until the workpiece touches the outer stop.

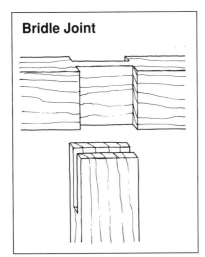

Bridle Joint

Bridle joint

The bridle joint is used in furniture making to join an intermediate leg on a table base to its apron. The leg section at the apron can be either flush or proud. The bridle joint is stronger than the lap joint because it has shoulders and twice as much glue area.

The cuts on the apron are made in the same way as a cross lap. However, you need to cut a lap on both sides of the board, so the depth of each lap should be no more than one-third the thickness of the workpiece. To cut the slot on the table leg, I use a shopmade tenoning jig (see the drawing below) and my sliding crosscut box. Clamp the on-end workpiece to the jig and then the whole assembly to the fence of the crosscut box, as shown in the photo at left.

I made a simple guard for the crosscut box that allows me to use the tenoning jig without compromising safety. The Lexan guard rides in the two grooves in the back of the crosscut box and is cut out in the front to accommodate the jig and workpiece.

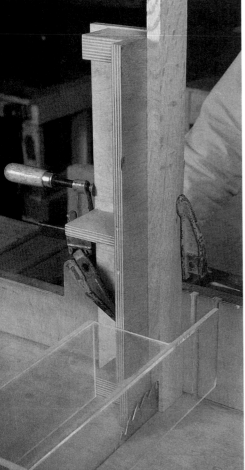

Cut the mortise for a bridle joint or open mortise and tenon using a tenoning jig clamped to the sliding crosscut box.

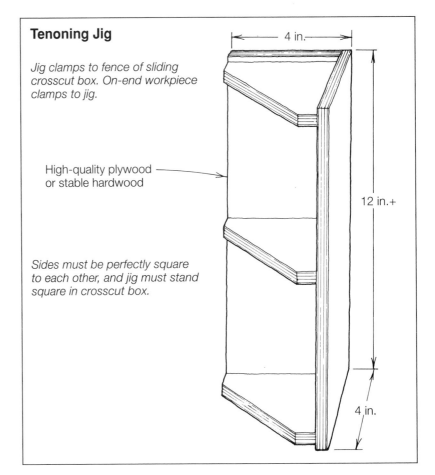

Tenoning Jig

Jig clamps to fence of sliding crosscut box. On-end workpiece clamps to jig.

4 in.

High-quality plywood or stable hardwood

12 in.+

Sides must be perfectly square to each other, and jig must stand square in crosscut box.

4 in.

Open mortise and tenon

The open mortise and tenon is the same as the bridle joint, except that the tenon is cut on the end of the crosspiece, not in the middle. Cut the mortise for the open mortise and tenon as you would the slot for the bridle joint. The tenon can be cut with table-sawn shoulders and routed cheeks (see pp. 165-166), or entirely on the table saw by clamping the board to the tenoning jig to cut the cheeks.

Mortise and tenon

The mortise-and-tenon joint is one of the strongest and most versatile frame joints in the furniture maker's repertory. It's certainly the joint that I use the most in my work. Variations on the simple tenon include the haunched tenon, through-wedged tenon, stub tenon, twin tenons, multiple tenons, and bare-faced tenons. Most of these tenons can be cut on the table saw using the same setup as for a simple tenon. Mortises, however, cannot be cut on the table saw; they are usually drilled out or routed and chiseled square.

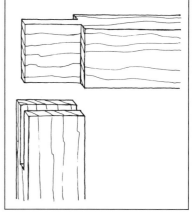

Open Mortise and Tenon

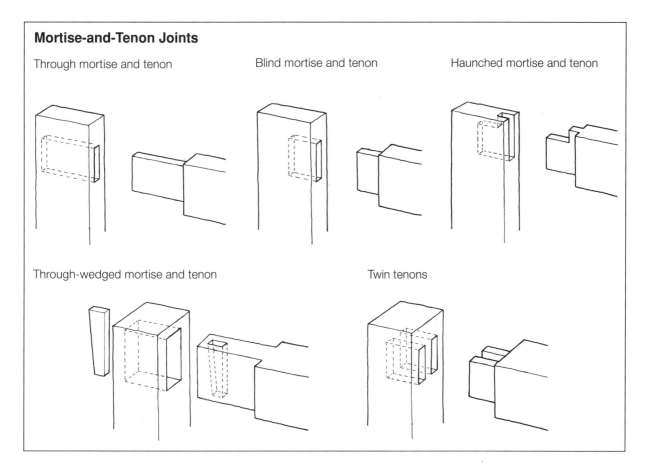

Mortise-and-Tenon Joints

Through mortise and tenon

Blind mortise and tenon

Haunched mortise and tenon

Through-wedged mortise and tenon

Twin tenons

There are many ways to cut a tenon. In school I learned to cut tenons by hand with a backsaw and chisel. Then when I was an apprentice at the assembly station of a small furniture factory, tenons came to me from a tenoning machine for final fitting to their mortises. My job consisted of sawing off the extra width and then paring the shoulders flat with a chisel. In my own shop, I started out using a router to cut the tenon cheeks, a bandsaw to cut the width and get close to the shoulder, and a chisel to finish the edge shoulders. Now I make tenons using the table saw and router, with final fitting done by hand.

Multiple-pass method

One of the simplest ways to cut tenons on the table saw is to make a series of passes on either side of the workpiece. The process is the same whether you are using a sliding crosscut box or a miter gauge. To set up for the multiple-pass method, clamp a stop the required distance from the blade and make the first cut (the shoulder) with the end of the workpiece butted against the stop. Move the workpiece a tad away from the stop and make repeated cuts until one side of the tenon is cut. Flip the piece and repeat. For a four-faced tenon, stand the workpiece on edge and cut the required amount from each side.

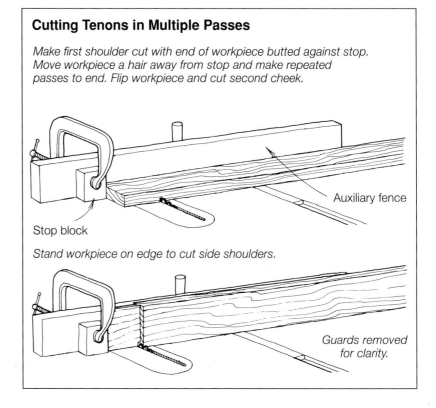

Cutting Tenons in Multiple Passes

Make first shoulder cut with end of workpiece butted against stop. Move workpiece a hair away from stop and make repeated passes to end. Flip workpiece and cut second cheek.

Auxiliary fence

Stop block

Stand workpiece on edge to cut side shoulders.

Guards removed for clarity.

The multiple-pass method is practical only when one or two tenons need to be cut. The point of the saw teeth will make for a rough tenon that will almost certainly require hand fitting to the exact thickness of the mortise.

On-end tenoning

Tenons can be cut with the workpiece standing on end using the tenoning jig. You can make the cut with a single sawblade, flipping the workpiece for the second cut, or with two sawblades and a spacer (see p. 156). Either method is suitable only for pieces that are short enough to handle on end — you clearly wouldn't want to attempt tenoning a bed rail using the tenoning jig. Once the cheeks are cut, the shoulders are cut as described below.

Combined method

My preferred method of cutting tenons involves three steps: crosscutting the shoulders on the table saw; routing the cheeks on a router table; and rounding the edges of the tenon to fit a routed mortise.

To cut the face shoulders, set the blade height and make test cuts on both sides of a scrap piece to make sure that the remaining center is the size of the mortise (standard tenon thickness is from one-third to one-half the thickness of the workpiece). Then clamp a stop block to

Clamp a stop block to the sliding crosscut box the length of the tenon from the blade and cut the tenon shoulders.

the sliding crosscut box, setting it to cut the shoulders at the tenon's exact length, which should be $\frac{1}{32}$ in. shorter than the mortise to allow for excess glue. Once all the face shoulders are cut, leave the stop block in place—you'll use it to cut the edge shoulders.

To rout the cheeks, use a $\frac{3}{4}$-in. dia. straight bit in a router table adjusted to match the height of the saw kerf. As always, verify the setup on a test piece. Set the router-table fence so that the bit cuts just short of the shoulder to avoid side-grain tearout.

To cut the edge shoulders, return the workpiece to the crosscut box and adjust the blade to the correct height (using the precut mortise as a reference). Cut with the work on edge. Once the edge shoulders are cut, the tenons can be cut to width with a bandsaw or by hand.

Finally, round the tenon's corners so it will fit the routed mortise. Chamfer the corners with a chisel, then sand them round with a strip of coarse sanding cloth. Clean up the corners near the shoulders with a chisel and fit the tenon to its mortise.

Cutting pegs for tenons

I reinforce almost all my mortise-and-tenon joints with square pegs, which I rip on the table saw from the edges of long stock. I choose material for pegs that has straight grain and ideally is denser than the wood it is going into. The stock you cut the peg material from must be square, at least on the faces that meet the table and the fence. Otherwise, the peg will be out of square and therefore undersized.

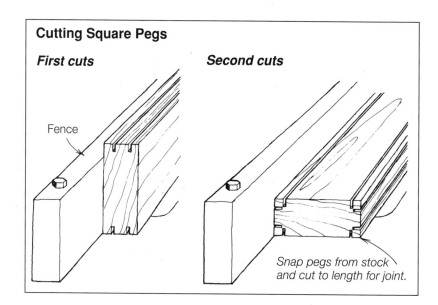

Cutting Square Pegs

First cuts

Second cuts

Fence

Snap pegs from stock and cut to length for joint.

To make the peg cross-section match the size of the drilled hole, I use the same drill bit to set the rip fence. Use a shopmade throat plate (see p. 61) since a standard one will swallow up the pegs.

Cutting pegs is a two-step operation. The first series of cuts are made along both edges of the piece; the second, along both faces. I set the blade height just below the height of the drill bit, which prevents the peg material from coming loose from the stock on the second cut and shooting from the saw. Begin by standing the workpiece on edge and cutting all four outside edges; make the second series of cuts with the face of the workpiece flat on the saw table (see the drawing on the facing page). The square peg material can then be snapped loose from the stock and cut to length for the joints. Some people fit a square peg in a round hole, but I generally square up the hole first with a chisel.

Finger joints

When I first started my furniture-making business, I used finger joints a lot for boxes, drawers and other production work. Finger joints appealed to me because the large glue surface area made for a particularly strong joint and the contrast between the end grain and face grain added an interesting decorative feature.

Although I no longer rely so heavily on finger joints, I do still use them in my work. Finger joints are made by cutting a series of equally spaced interlocking slots and fingers into the ends of mating pieces. For the pieces to interlock, the joint of one piece must begin with a finger, and the joint of the mating piece with a slot.

You should size your stock to get full-width fingers or slots across the board, especially if the finger is only a single blade-kerf wide. Check the dimensions before you begin by dividing the board's width by the width of the saw kerf. With wider joints cut with a dado head instead of a sawblade, you can adjust the width of the cutter before you begin so the slots and fingers will cover the width of the board.

To cut finger joints I use a jig clamped to the fence of my crosscut box or onto a miter gauge (see the sidebar on p. 168). The jig provides a guide for stepping off the fingers and slots as you move the stock through the blade. The key to successful finger-jointing is to locate the jig precisely one saw kerf away from the far side of the blade. You may have to do some fiddling to get it right, but even a slight error will compound across the width of a board to ruin the joint. Here's where your test pieces come in handy. Cut a few fingers on the ends of two

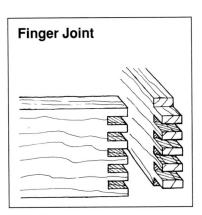

Finger Joint

*F*inger-joint jig

A simple finger-joint jig can be made from a plywood board with a slot in one edge that corresponds to the slots you want to make in the workpieces, and a hardwood key or metal pin that fits snugly in the slots and indexes the cuts. I usually make the slot a standard blade kerf wide, but for wider slots you can use a dado cutter. The height of the jig isn't critical, but if you're using it in the sliding crosscut box it's nice to make it fairly high in the middle to give more support to the pieces held upright for the end-grain cuts. To cut the slot in the jig, adjust the height of the blade to slightly

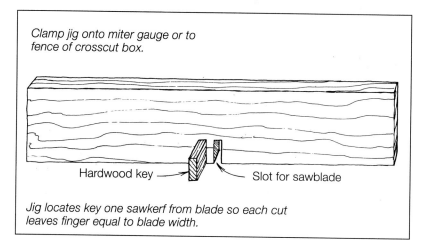

Clamp jig onto miter gauge or to fence of crosscut box.

Hardwood key ——→   ←—— Slot for sawblade

Jig locates key one sawkerf from blade so each cut leaves finger equal to blade width.

less than the thickness of the pieces that you are cutting. Push the jig over the blade to make a slot, and glue in a key that is long enough to extend well into the workpiece. Chamfer the top edges and sand the sides lightly for a snug fit.

I made a guard for the jig that stops short of the front fence of the crosscut box; a piece of wood attached to the rear of the guard is used to clamp the guard to the rear fence (see the photo at top on the facing page).

scraps and see how and if they fit together. A nice easy fit, neither too tight nor too loose, is what you are looking for. If the joint is off, move the jig one way or the other until the fit is perfect.

Now re-adjust the blade so it protrudes above the table about $\frac{1}{32}$ in. more than the thickness of the stock being joined. The end grain of the fingers will suck up glue and it will be easier to sand or plane the tips off than to level the full length of the sides. I use a 50-tooth combination blade, which leaves only a slight crown at the top of the joint that it is difficult to notice after glue-up. It is important to lock in the blade height so that all cuts remain the same height. If you are using the miter gauge instead of a crosscut box, also check that the throat plate is level.

Ideally, each joint should start and end with the same element, either a slot or a finger. This isn't absolutely necessary, but it lets you flip each piece end-for-end and cut both sides at the same time with the same setup. I always cut the first piece so that the joint begins with a finger. That way you can butt the piece against the key, and the positive stop of the key eliminates having to align the stock with the kerf in the support board the first time the jig is used.

Finger joints can be cut on the table saw using a simple jig fitted with a metal pin or hardwood key. The first cut is made with the edge of the workpiece against the pin. Subsequent cuts are made by placing the last-cut slot over the pin. The first slot cut in the mating board uses the last-cut finger on the first piece to establish the correct spacing.

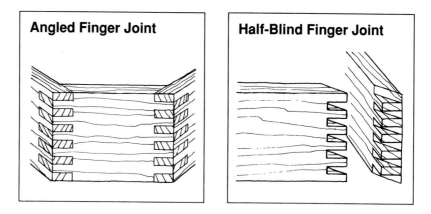

Angled Finger Joint

Half-Blind Finger Joint

After cutting the first slot, which simultaneously creates the first finger, I move the board so the new slot can be slid down on the key and the next slot-finger pair can be cut. The process is repeated until the fingers and slots extend across the width of the board. After completing the joint half that began with a finger, I use the first finger on the piece as a stop to cut the first slot on the mating piece.

Angled finger joint
In order to gain maximum depth and width for the drawer in a corner cupboard you can make a polygon that follows the inside angles of the cupboard, and join the sides with angled finger joints. The setup for cutting these joints is the same as for standard finger joints, except that the jig is tilted to reflect the joint angle. The ends of the boards to be joined are cut at the same angle.

Half-blind finger joint
Half-blind finger joints are concealed from the front and visible from the side. For this joint, cut the fingers on the side piece as for a standard finger joint and the fingers on the front piece angled at 45°, leaving the end of the piece at 90°. The side piece then gets cut at 45° even with the outside edge.

Miter joints

Miters are end-grain joints that are quite common in both frame and carcase construction, but they have little strength and must be reinforced, even when you can get them to fit perfectly, which is no small task. Sometimes miters have decorative design value — they show no end grain, and if matched well will lead the eye around corners easily. I've had very little reason to cut miters in my furniture work, so it's not a joint I have tried to perfect. I have used forms of the miter joint for picture frames, ogee feet and molding.

Some miter-joint variations are the spline edge miter, the slip feather (spline miter) and the mock finger joint. The miters themselves can be cut on the table saw as described on pp. 136-139; cutting the variations is described below.

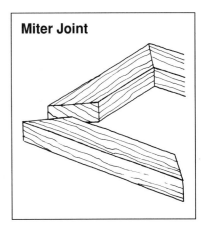

Miter Joint

Spline edge miter

A spline edge miter has a long spline crossing the joint at an angle to the corner. To cut the slots for a spline edge miter, tilt the blade so that the blade angle added to the angle in the work equals 90°. For a standard 45° miter tilt the blade to 45°, as shown in the drawing at left below. For ¾-in. thick material, a ⅛-in. thick spline is adequate. Placing the groove close to the inside edge allows you to use a wider spline, which makes for a stronger joint. Use the miter gauge and the rip fence as a stop, or a cutoff box and a stop.

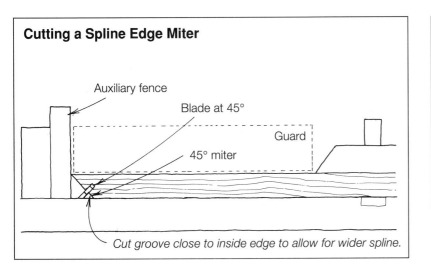

Cutting a Spline Edge Miter

Auxiliary fence

Blade at 45°

Guard

45° miter

Cut groove close to inside edge to allow for wider spline.

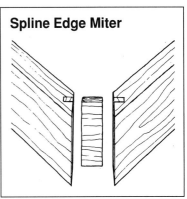

Spline Edge Miter

*J*ig for slip feather joint

The jig holds a frame on edge at a 45° angle to the sawblade. The jig is made by attaching two 1½-in. to 2-in. boards at 45° to a flat piece of plywood, as shown in the drawing at right. Trim the two boards at 45°, flush with the bottom of the jig, so the sawblade doesn't need to be raised too high to slot the frame. A facing board attached across the two angled pieces can serve as a guard and also add some stability, though I usually prefer to use a guard fence clamped to the saw table instead.

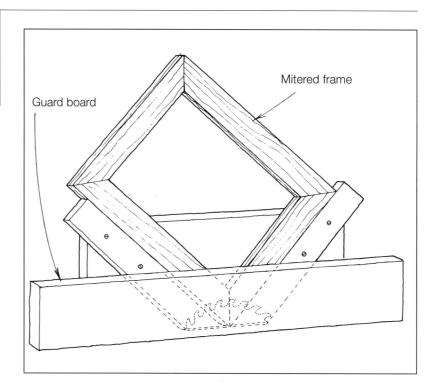

Guard board

Mitered frame

Slip Feather

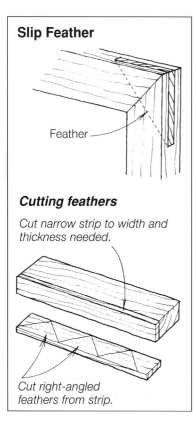

Feather

Cutting feathers

Cut narrow strip to width and thickness needed.

Cut right-angled feathers from strip.

Slip feather

The slip feather, or spline miter, is used to reinforce a mitered frame. The slot for the spline is cut after the frame has been mitered and glued up. Place the glued frame in a jig (see the sidebar above) and raise the blade so that it will cut just short of the inside corner. For a narrow frame, adjust the fence to make one centered slot (either a single blade kerf or a dado). A frame more than 1 in. wide requires two splines.

After making the slot, glue in a wooden spline. Slip-feather splines are easily made by cutting a narrow strip to the required width and thickness. Cut the splines at a double 45° with a miter gauge and extended auxiliary fence. Use a piece of masking tape on the saw table to gauge the length of the cuts (cut a little longer than you'll need). Cut to the mark and then turn the strip over.

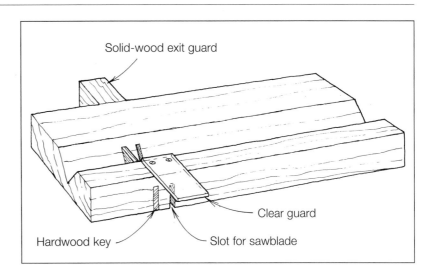

Solid-wood exit guard

Clear guard

Hardwood key

Slot for sawblade

Make a V-block jig from a piece of 2-in. thick stable stock at least 8 in. wide and about 16 in. long. Cut out the V-groove in two passes with the blade tilted at 45°. Leave at least ¼ in. between the point of the V and the bottom of the block, and position the groove so it is closer to one edge than to the other.

After the wedge has been removed, use the miter gauge to guide the V-block and cut a slot in the jig shy of the top and shorter than the height of the spline needed for the box you want to make. Next cut a hardwood key that will fit snugly into the slot, just as you did for the finger-joint jig (see p. 168). Move the jig over a distance equal to the spacing you want between slots, and make a second cut. The spacing can be equal to the width of the splines, as in the finger joint, or you can leave larger spaces between the splines. Finally, attach a clear guard to the front of the jig and a solid-wood guard at the rear.

Mock finger joint

The mock finger joint looks a lot like a finger joint but is actually a form of the spline miter. This joint is used on wider, box-type frames and requires a different jig (see the sidebar above) than the one used for spline miter joints.

The slots for the mock finger joint are cut after the box has been mitered and glued up. Position one corner of the box in the V-block jig, with its edge against the hardwood key, and cut the first slot. Move the box over so the slot fits over the key and make the second cut, just as you did with the finger-joint jig. Continue across the piece until all the slots are cut. Complete the joint by gluing in the splines.

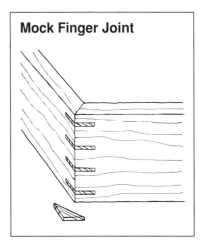

Mock Finger Joint

SOURCES OF SUPPLY

The following companies sell table saws, sawblades, various accessories and safety equipment, either through distributors or mail order. Many offer a catalog; call or write for cost and other information.

Airflow Systems
11370 Pagemill Drive
Dallas, TX 75243
(214) 272-3003
Dust collectors

Amana Tool Corp.
120 Carolyn Boulevard
Farmingdale, NY 11735
(800) 445-0077
(516) 752-1300
Sawblades

American Machine & Tool
Fourth and Spring Streets
Royersford, PA 19468
(215) 948-0400
Table saws

The Belsaw Company
4111 Central Avenue N.E.
Minneapolis, MN 55421
(800) 468-4449
(612) 781-2345
Table saws and accessories

**Biesemeyer
Manufacturing Corp.**
216 South Alma School Road
Mesa, AZ 85202
(800) 782-1831
Replacement rip fences, replacement blade guards, extension tables, sliding crosscut tables

Bilsom Group
109 Carpenter Drive
Sterling, VA 20164
(800) 733-1177
Ear, eye and face protectors

Black & Decker U.S.
626 Hanover Pike
Hampstead, MD 21074
(410) 239-5300
Table saws, sawblades

Bridge City Tool Works
1104 N.E. 28th Avenue
(800) 253-3332
Portland, OR 97232
Layout tools, safety accessories

Cabot Safety Corp.
5457 W. 79th Street
Indianapolis, IN 46268
(800) 225-9038
Ear, eye, face and respiratory protectors

Chiswick Trading Co.
33 Union Avenue
Sudbury, MA 01776-0907
(800) 225-8708
Rubber fatigue mats, plastic dust-collector bags, aprons and safety clothing

Davis & Wells
11090 S. Alameda Street
Lynwood, CA 90262
(213) 636-0621
Industrial table saws, used saws

Delta International
246 Alpha Drive
Pittsburgh, PA 15238
(800) 438-2486
(800) 438-2487 (in Pennsylvania)
Table saws and accessories, sawblades, dust collectors, power feeders

Direct Safety Company
7815 S. 46th Street
Phoenix, AZ 85044
(800) 528-7405
Safety supplies

**Everlast Saw &
Carbide Tools**
9 Otis Street
West Babylon, NY 11704
(800) 828-7297
(516) 491-1900
Carbide sawblades

Excalibur Machine & Tool Co.
210 Eighth Street South
Lewiston, NY 14092
(800) 387-9789
Replacement rip fences, replacement blade guards

Forrest Manufacturing Co.
461 River Road
Clifton, NJ 07014
(800) 733-7111
Sawblades (sharpening and repair service also available)

Freud
P.O. Box 7187
High Point, NC 27264
(800) 472-7307
Sawblades

F.S. Tool Corp.
210 Eighth Street South
Lewiston, NY 14092
(800) 387-9723
Sawblades

Garrett Wade Company
161 Avenue of the Americas
New York, NY 10013
(800) 221-2942
(212) 807-1155
Inca table saws (East Coast), table-saw accessories, layout tools, safety equipment

General: J. Philip Humfrey Ltd.
3241 Kennedy Road, Unit 7
Scarborough, Ontario, Canada
(800) 387-9789
Table saws and accessories

General Saw Corp.
20 Wood Avenue
Secaucus, NJ 07096-1365
(201) 867-5330
Sawblades

Greenlee Textron
4455 Boeing Drive
Rockford, IL 61109
(800) 435-0786 (sales)
(800) 435-2932 (service)
(815) 397-7070
Sawblades (and sharpening service)

Grizzly Imports
East Coast: 2406 Reach Road
Williamsport, PA 17701
(800) 523-4777
West Coast: P.O. Box 2069
Bellingham, WA 98227
(800) 541-5537
Table saws, dust collectors, power feeders

Harbor Freight Tools
3491 Mission Oaks Boulevard
Camarillo, CA 93011-6010
(800) 423-2567
Dust collectors, discount table saws

Hitachi Power Tools USA
3950 Steve Reynolds Blvd.
Norcross, GA 30093
(800) 598-6657
Table saws

HTC Products
120 East Hudson
P.O. Box 839
Royal Oak, MI 48068-0839
(800) 624-2027
Brett-Guard, outfeed supports, mobile table-saw bases

Industrial Safety & Security
1390 Neubrecht Road
Lima, OH 45801
(419) 227-6030
Safety supplies

Injecta Machinery
2217 El Sol Avenue
Altadena, CA 91001
(818) 797-8262
Inca table saws and accessories (West Coast)

Jet Equipment & Tools
P.O. Box 1477
Tacoma, WA 98401-1477
(800) 274-6848
Table saws, dust collectors, power feeders

Kenco Safety Products
70 Rock City Road
Woodstock, NY 12498
(800) 341-4103
Safety supplies

Lab Safety Supply
P.O. Box 1368
Janesville, WI 53547-1368
(800) 356-0783
(800) 356-2501 (technical advice)
Safety supplies

Laguna Tools
2081 Laguna Canyon Road
Laguna Beach, CA 92651
(800) 234-1976
(714) 494-7006
Robland table saws, dust collectors, sliding tables

Leichtung Workshops
4944 Commerce Parkway
Cleveland, OH 44128
(800) 321-6840
Hold-down wheels

Leitz Tooling Systems
4301 East Paris S.E.
Grand Rapids, MI 49512
(616) 698-7010
Sawblades

Lobo Power Tools
9031 East Slauson Avenue
Pico Rivera, CA 90660
(800) 786-5626
(310) 949-3747
Table saws, power feeders

Makita USA
14930 Northam Street
La Mirada, CA 90638
(310) 926-8775
Table saws

Peltor
Peltor Park
41 Commercial Way
East Providence, RI 02914
(800) 327-6833
Hearing protectors

Powermatic Corporation
Morrison Road
McMinnville, TN 37110
(800) 248-0144
Table saws and accessories,
sawblades

Primark Tool Group
1350 S. 15th Street
Louisville, KY 40210
(800) 233-7297
(502) 635-8100
Sawblades

Quintec
P.O. Box 736
Newberg, OR 97132
(800) 423-9611
Paralok replacement rip fence

Racal Health & Safety
7305 Executive Way
Frederick, MD 21701-8368
(800) 682-9500
Head, eye, face and respiratory
protectors

Ryobi America Corporation
5201 Pearman Dairy Road
Anderson, SC 29625-8950
(800) 525-2579
Table saws

Sears Roebuck and Co.
P.O. Box 19009
Provo, UT 84605-9009
(800) 377-7414
Catalog tool sales

Shophelper Ltd.
323 West Cromwell #118
Fresno, CA 93711
(800) 344-7455
Shophelper anti-kickback wheels

Shopsmith
3931 Image Drive
Dayton, OH 45414-2591
(800) 762-7555
(513) 898-6070
Shopsmith combination table saw,
safety accessories

Skil Corporation
4300 West Peterson Avenue
Chicago, IL 60646
(800) 621-5143
8-in. table saw

L.S. Starrett Co.
121 Crescent Street
Athol, MA 01331
(508) 249-3551
Squares and layout tools

Sunhill Machinery
500 Andover Park East
Seattle, WA 98188
(800) 929-4321
Table saws, dust collectors, power
feeders

Systi Matic Company
12530 135th Avenue N.E.
Kirkland, WA 98034
(800) 426-0000
Sawblades

Trend-Lines
375 Beacham Street
P.O. Box 6447
Chelsea, MA 02150-0999
(800) 767-9999
(617) 884-8882
Table saws and accessories,
sawblades, safety supplies

Vega Enterprises
R.R. #3 Box 193
Decatur, IL 62526
(800) 222-8342
Replacement rip fences, table saws,
sliding tables

Wilke Machinery Co.
3230 Susquehanna Trail
York, PA 17402
(717) 764-5000
Bridgewood table saws, dust
collectors, power feeders

Woodcraft
210 Wood County Industrial Park
P.O. Box 1686
Parkersburg, WV 26102-1686
(800) 225-1153
Sawblades, accessories, safety
supplies

The Woodworkers' Store
21801 Industrial Boulevard
Rogers, MN 55374-9514
(612) 428-3200
Accessories, safety supplies

Woodworker's Supply
5604 Alameda Place, NE
Albuquerque, NM 87113-2100
(800) 645-9292
Table saws and accessories,
sawblades

York Saw & Knife Co.
P.O. Box 733
York, PA 17405
(800) 654-7297
Sawblades (and sharpening service)

INDEX

A

Accuracy: relative vs. absolute, 100
Anti-kickback fingers: described, 14, 76
Aprons, shop: recommended, 47
Arbor assembly:
 described, 11-12
 flange of, truing, 62
 maintaining, 62
 shaft of, aligning with motor shaft, 64-65
 testing, 17

B

Base: *See* Saw base.
Bearings:
 maintaining, 62
 oiling, 67
 testing, 17
Belts: *See* V-belts.
Bench saws: described, 4
Bevels:
 crosscutting, 135-136
 ripping, 116
Bevels, sliding: table-saw uses for, 46
Blade guards:
 about, 13, 76
 after-market replacement, 76-80
 BladeGuard (Biesemeyer), 78
 Brett-Guard (HTC), 77-78
 Excalibur Overarm Sawblade Cover, 79
 sources for, 174-176
 Uniguard (Delta), 79
 for grooving cuts, 144
 for rabbet cuts, 150, 151
 for ripping narrow stock, 110, 111
 for sliding crosscut box, 124, 126, 162
 standard, limitations of, 76
Blades: *See* Sawblades.
Bridle joint: cutting, 162
Butt joint: cutting, 142-143

C

Cabinet saws: described, 5
Calipers: table-saw uses for, 46
Carts: wheeled, 43-44
Clothing: for shop wear, 47, 72, 103
Collars, flanged: *See* Sawblades, stiffeners for.
Contractor's saws: described, 4-5
Coves:
 cutting, 117-119
 parallelogram jig for, 117, 118
Cradle assembly: described, 11
Crosscutting:
 auxiliary fence for, 121, 122-123
 bevels, 135-136
 blades for, 24, 127
 long stock, 133
 miter gauge for, 120-122
 miters, 136
 repetitive, 129-132
 safety considerations for, 120, 123
 short pieces, 134
 stance for, 128-129
 standard procedure for, 127-129
 stop blocks for, 129-131
 wide panels, 133-134
 See also Sliding crosscut box.

D

Dado crosscut box: in use, 154
Dadoes:
 blades for, 26-28
 blind, cutting, 155-156
 corner, 157
 cutting, 151-158
 dovetail, 158
 housed, cutting, 153, 155
 See also Grooves. Lap joints. Rabbets. Tongue and dado.
Dial indicator: for measuring runout, 62-63
Dust:
 hazards of exposure to, 85-86
 protection against, 86-87
 See also Dust collection.

Dust collection:
 need for, 37
 sealing up the saw for, 38
 systems for, 37-40, 86
 choosing, 39-40
 single-stage vs. two-stage, 39-40
 sources for, 174-176

E

Edge joints:
 butt, 142-143
 hidden spline, 146
 splined, 143-144
 tongue and groove, 156
End miters: *See* Bevels, crosscutting.
Extension tables: *See* Outfeed supports.
Eye protection:
 goggles for, 90
 need for, 88
 safety glasses for, 89-90

F

Featherboards:
 for grooving cuts, 144
 against kickback, 80-81, 144
 for rabbet cuts, 151
Fences:
 auxiliary, for crosscutting, 121, 122-123
 auxiliary, for ripping, 94-95
 for cutting coves, 117, 118
 for cutting miters, 137
 for cutting rabbets, 149-150
 extended, 95, 107
 half-, 95-97
 high, 95
 low, 95, 109
 for miter gauge, making, 122
 See also Rip fences.
Fingerboards:
 See Featherboards.
Finger joints:
 angled, 170
 cutting, 167-169
 jig for, 141, 168
 half-blind, 170
 mock finger, 173

Fire extinguisher: need for in workshop, 91
First aid:
 books on, 90
 for eye injuries, 89
 kit, for workshop, 91

G

Grooves:
 blades for, 26-28
 stopped, cutting, 146-147
 through, cutting, 144-145
 See also Dadoes.
Guards: *See* Blade guards.

H

Handwheels: for blade adjustment, 10
Health hazards: *See* Dust. Eye protection. Noise.
Hearing protectors:
 sources for, 174-176
 types of, 84-85
 See also Noise.
"Helpers": for ripping long stock, 105
Hold-down wheels:
 against kickback, 80-81
 sources for, 174-176

J

Jigs:
 for cutting coves, 117-119
 for finger joint, 141, 167, 168
 for mock finger joint, 173
 for ripping irregular stock, 115
 for ripping narrow stock, 110, 111
 for ripping tapers, 115
 for slip feather joint, 172
 for tenoning, 162
 V-block for cutting corners, 157
Joinery:
 blades for, 142
 edge, 142-148
 and glue-joint strength, 140, 142
 marking system for, 145

safety considerations with, 143
test pieces for, 160
See also specific joints.

K

Kickback:
  anti-kickback fingers
    against, 14, 72, 76
  causes of, 70-74, 95
  correct ripping technique
    against, 74
  with dado blades, 27, 155
  defined, 70
  featherboard against, 80
  half-fence against, 72, 95-97
  hold-down wheels against,
    80-81
  splitter against, 13, 72,
    73, 74
  and thick stock, 113

L

Lap joints:
  cross, cutting, 161
  edge, 159
  end, cutting, 159-160
  T-lap, 159
  See also Bridle joint.
    Mortise-and-tenon
    joints, open.
Lighting: of work area, 34
Lubricants: for saw parts, 67

M

Maintenance: *See individual
  saw components.*
Masking tape: table-saw
  uses for, 46
Measuring: tools for, 45-46
Micro-adjuster: for rip fence,
  101
Miter gauges:
  about, 9, 10, 120
  auxiliary fences for,
    122-123
  for cutting miters, 137
  eliminating play in, 52
  European-style, 10, 123
  replacement, 123
  setting, 59, 136
  standard, limitations of, 122
Miter-gauge slots:
  about, 10
  blade alignment with,
    49, 51-53

Miter joints:
  mock finger, 173
  slip feather, 172
    jig for, 172
  spline edge, 171
    jig for, 173
Miters:
  crosscutting, 136-139
    sliding crosscut box for,
      138-139
    stops for, 138
Molding:
  bevel crosscuts for, 135
  cutters for, 29
  See also Coves.
Mortise-and-tenon joints:
  open, 163
  pegs for, 166-167
  types of, 163
Motor: adjusting, 65

N

Noise:
  hearing destruction by,
    83, 84
  measure of, 83
  protection from, 83-85

O

Outfeed supports:
  commercial, 41-42
    sources for, 174-176
  with long stock, 104-105
  as safety accessory, 83
  with sheet stock, 107-109
  shopmade, 41-42
  with wide panels, 133

P

Pawls, anti-kickback: *See*
  Anti-kickback fingers.
Pegs: for tenons, cutting,
  166-167
Plywood:
  blades for, 24, 26, 108
  cutting, 107-109
  for splines, 146
Power feeders:
  for ripping, 83
  sources for, 174-176
Pulleys:
  aligning, 64-65
  guard for, 14
Pushers:
  to prevent kickback, 74
  and ripping, 103, 111, 112
  types of, 81-82

R

Rabbets:
  cutting with dado blade,
    151-152
  cutting with single blade,
    148-150
  edge tongue and groove,
    156
  full tongue and dado, 156
  See also Dadoes. Lap joints.
Rack gears:
  described, 12
  lubricating, 67
Rails:
  described, 8
  See also Rip fences,
    replacement.
Raised panels: *See* Coves.
Resawing: on table saw,
  disadvised, 114
Rip fences:
  about, 8, 9
  aligning, 56-57, 92
  auxiliary, 94-95
  micro-adjuster for, 101
  replacement, 8, 97-99
    Biesemeyer, 97, 99
    Excalibur, 98
    rails of, 99
    sources for, 174-176
    Vega, 98
  setting, 74, 92, 94, 100-101
  shimming, 56
  standard, limitations of, 94
  See also Ripping.
Ripping:
  at an angle, 115
  bevels, 116
  blade height for, 100
  blades for, 24, 25, 100
  irregular stock, 114-115
  and kickback, 72
  long stock, 104-106
  making the cut, 102
  narrow stock, 109-111
  safe procedure for, 74,
    100-104
  sheet stock, 107-109
  short pieces, 111, 134
  stance for, 102-104, 106, 108
  thick stock, 112-113
  thin stock, 112
  unsurfaced boards, 116
  See also Rip fences.
Riving knives: *See* Splitters.
Rulers: table-saw uses for, 46
Runout:
  about, 22
  in arbor flange, 62
  in blade, 63

S

Safety:
  attitudes toward, 68
  general guidelines for,
    72-73
  See also Kickback. Safety
    accessories.
Safety accessories:
  anti-kickback fingers, 14, 76
  belt and pulley guard, 14
  blade guard, 13, 76-80
  featherboards, 80-81
  guards for crosscut box,
    124, 126, 162
  half-fence, 95
  hold-down wheels, 80-81
  knee switch, 36
  pushers, 81-82
  sources for, 174-176
  splitters, 13, 74-75
  *See also individual
    accessories.*
Safety wheels: *See* Hold-down
  wheels.
Saw base:
  about, 6
  leveling, 50
Sawblades:
  aligning to miter-gauge slot,
    49, 51-53
  aligning with splitter, 58
  angle of, changing, 10
  arbor hole in, 22
  body of, 21-22
  carbide vs. steel, 20
  changing, 19, 23, 28
  checking 45° setting, 55
  checking 90° setting,
    53-54, 55
  cleaning, 31
  combination, 24, 26
  consumer-grade, 20
  contractor-grade, 20
  for crosscutting, 24, 25,
    127
  for cutting coves, 117
  for cutting plywood, 24,
    26, 108
  dado, 26-28
    adjustable, 27
    installing, 28
    stacking, 26-27
  height of, changing, 10
  hollow-ground, 21
  industrial-grade, 18
  maintenance of, 30-31
  for ripping, 24, 25, 100
  runout of, 22
    measuring, 63
  sources for, 174-176

stiffeners for, 29-30
storage box for, 44, 45
thin-kerf, 22, 30, 112
See also Sawteeth.
Saw table:
about, 8
cleaning, 66
extensions for, 8, 50
leveling, 50
See also Outfeed supports.
Sawteeth:
carbide-tipped, 20
grinds of,
alternate-top bevel, 25
alternate-top bevel and
raker, 26
flat-top, 25
triple-chip, 26
set of, 20-21
Sheet stock:
cutting, 107-109
extended fence for, 107
Shop accessories:
carts, 43-44
drums, 44
storage racks, 44
Sliding crosscut box:
for cutting cross-lap joint,
161
for cutting finger joints,
141, 167-169
for cutting long stock, 133
for cutting tenon shoulders,
165-166
for cutting wide panels,
133-134
fence for, 125
extensions for, 132
guard for, 124, 126
making, 125-126
for repetitive crosscutting,
131-132
for standard crosscutting,
128
stop blocks for, 126
Spline joints:
hidden spline, 146-148
splined edge, 143-145
splines for, 146, 172
Spline miter joint: *See* Miter
joints, slip feather.
Splitters:
about, 13
aligning with blade, 58
against kickback, 72, 73, 74
squaring to table, 58
types of, 74-75
Spreaders: *See* Splitters.
Squares:
table-saw uses for, 45
testing, 46

Stock preparation: discussed,
92, 94
Stop blocks:
for cutting grooves,
147-148
for cutting miters, 136
FastTrack system for, 132
on miter-gauge auxiliary
fence, 130
for repetitive crosscutting,
129
for tenoning, 164-165
Switches:
knee, 10, 36
magnetic vs. toggle, 11
placement of, 10

T

Table: *See* Saw table.
Table insert: *See* Throat plate.
Table saws:
bench, 4
cabinet, 5
choosing, 14-17
cleaning, 66-67
contractor's, 4-5
dust collection at, 37-40
guidelines for safe
operation of, 72-73
horsepower requirements
for, 15-16
industrial, 6
internal assembly of, 11-12
lighting requirements for,
34
lubricating, 66-67
motorized vs.
motor-driven, 4
shop accessories for, 41-44
shop placement of, 32-35
shop tools for, 45-46
size of, 4, 14
sources for, 174-176
tuning, 48-65
used, buying, 17
weight of, 15
wiring requirements for,
34-35
Tearout: minimizing, 28,
107-108
Tenons:
cutting, 164-166
on end, 165
jig for, 162
in multiple passes,
164-165
shoulders, 165-166
fitting, 166
pegs for, 166-167
router for, 166

Throat plate:
about, 10
for dado blade, 28, 151
for flanged collar, 30
leveling, 60
to minimize tearout, 107
wooden, making, 61
Tongue and dado:
bare-faced, 152-153
full, 156
Tongue and groove:
See Edge joints.
Tools:
for measuring and
marking, 45
sources for, 174-176
Trunnions:
about, 11
lubricating, 67

V

V-belts:
adjusting, 64
guard for, 14
replacing, 64

W

Wiring: for table saw, 34-35
Wood:
drying defects in, and
kickback, 71-72
natural flaws in, and
kickback, 71
Workshop:
setting up for table-saw
operation, 32-34

Editors: RUTH DOBSEVAGE, ANDY SCHULTZ

Designer/Layout Artist: JODIE DELOHERY

Illustrator: LEE HOV

Photographer, except where noted: DICK BURROWS

Copy/Production Editor: PETER CHAPMAN

Art Assistant: ILIANA KOEHLER

Typeface: GARAMOND

Paper: WARREN PATINA MATTE, 70 lb., NEUTRAL pH

Printer: ARCATA GRAPHICS/HAWKINS, NEW CANTON, TENNESSEE

NEW...

Mastering Your Table Saw
with **Kelly Mehler**

A Fine Woodworking **Video Workshop**